The Family Treasury of
Jewish Holidays

The Family Treasury of

Jewish Holidays

by Malka Drucker

Illustrated by Nancy Patz

LITTLE, BROWN AND COMPANY
New York ⌇ Boston

The author would like to thank the following people for their collaboration in this book: Dr. Ron Wolfson for his generosity and cooperation; Ellen Bernstein for allowing me to borrow from her brilliant Tu B'Sh'vat Haggadah; Andrea Brown, agent and friend; the Stephanies—Owens Lurie and True—and Hannah Mahoney, who provided the best editorial help; Jonathan and Chris, my teachers; and always, Gay.

The illustrator extends her warmest thanks to: Susan L. Roth, for starting it all; Lilian M. C. Randall, research curator of manuscripts, Walters Art Gallery, Baltimore; Michael Grunberger, head of the Hebraic Section, Library of Congress; Peggy K. Pearlstein, area specialist, Library of Congress; Jean Katcoff, curator of periodicals, Baltimore Hebrew University Library; Virginia R. North, archivist, Jewish Historical Society, Baltimore; Rabbi Donald R. Berlin; Betsey Heuisler; Ann Zaiman; Joanne C. Fruchtman; Diana H. Green; David G. Schuchat — and with special appreciation, Jeannie, Peter, Susan, Alan, and Patrick.

Little, Brown and Company

Hachette Book Group USA
237 Park Avenue, New York, NY 10017
Visit our Web site at www.lb-kids.com

First Paperback Edition: September 1999

Copyright acknowledgments appear on page 180.

Library of Congress Cataloging-in-Publication Data

Drucker, Malka.
  The family treasury of Jewish holidays / by Malka Drucker ; illustrated by Nancy Patz.
    p.   cm.
  Summary: Recounts the history and rituals of ten Jewish holidays, including appropriate games, recipes, and songs.
    ISBN 978-0-316-19343-6 (hc)
    ISBN 978-0-316-19313-9 (pb)
    1. Fasts and feasts — Judaism — Juvenile literature.   2. Judaism — Customs and practices — Juvenile literature.   [1. Fasts and feasts — Judaism.   2. Judaism — Customs and practices.]   I. Patz, Nancy, ill.   II. Title.
    BM690.D77 1994
    296.4'3 — dc20   93-7549
              10 9 8 7 6 (pb)

IM

Printed in Singapore

The illustrations in this book were painted with transparent watercolors and inks, using brushes, pens, and quills, on 140-pound Fabrino 5 hot-pressed watercolor paper.

For my mother, who taught me
the magic of stories

M. D.

To the Hebrew manuscript painters of
centuries past — in tribute to their gifts

N. P.

Contents

 # Introduction

Malka Drucker and Dr. Ron Wolfson

"Why can't I eat bread during Passover?"

"Did the jug of oil for the menorah lamp really last eight days?"

"Can children light the candles on Friday night?"

According to Harvard professor Robert Coles, children have deeply felt spiritual needs that often go unnoticed or are undernourished by parents and teachers. The questions children ask about religious practices are clues to this youthful spirituality. Many adults, on the other hand, feel they lack spiritual awareness, perhaps because as children they were not encouraged to trust and explore the mysterious path of the holy.

When children ask us questions about the Jewish tradition, we may find ourselves stammering because we think we should know the answers, and often we don't. Their questions challenge our own unanswered questions about what we believe and what kind of Judaism we practice. Even when we know the answers, we are still unsure about what words to use. How do we talk to children about Judaism in a way that will interest them?

We found the answer in a most surprising, yet wonderful place: children's books. Here we found the information, values, and ideas we wanted to express, and best of all, we found a way to share them with our children — by reading aloud.

Children love to be read to; they often request the same story to be read over and over again. Parents who read to their children — at bedtime, at the dinner table, on holidays — are modeling one of the most crucial activities for intellectual development. Furthermore, families who read aloud ultimately create ardent readers.

Reading together also gives us the chance to share new knowledge, images, and even emotions with our children. The Jewish tradition says that parents bear the responsibility of teaching their children Torah, the ethical way to live. By choosing a story and reading it aloud, we become active participants in our children's moral education.

Listening to a riveting story will build anticipation for a holiday, encourage a wish for a Jewish life, and create sweet memories of reading together. In *The Family Treasury of Jewish Holidays*, we offer a sampling of our favorite stories, poems, and songs to help you celebrate the holidays with your children. Because we also want to move the experience from the heart and mind to the hand, we've included recipes, games, and crafts as well. And to help answer everyone's questions, you'll find explanations of the holidays, their traditions, and their symbols.

The holidays are a wonderful opportunity to give Jewish children a sense of belonging to a tradition that spans three thousand years and nearly every country in the world. The abundance of holidays not only helps us to feel and experience Judaism often, it also creates a steady anticipation throughout the year. As soon as Hanukkah ends, we look forward to planting trees on Tu B'Sh'vat, and, of course, every week brings sweet Shabbat, the Day of Rest.

This book is not only for children to read. It is also for *you* — parent, grandparent, or friend — to share with children. Read the stories aloud as you prepare for a holiday, during the celebration itself, and at bedtime on the night of a festival. These stories offer special meaning when they are encountered together — and together, families and friends will share the joys of Jewish holiday celebration.

The Family Treasury of

Jewish Holidays

Rosh Hashanah
and Yom Kippur

Rosh Hashanah *and* Yom Kippur

Sweet Beginnings

Rosh Hashanah and Yom Kippur are the holiest days of the Jewish year. They are also the most difficult to understand because, unlike other holidays, they don't celebrate a season or an important historical event. Instead they celebrate something intensely personal and extraordinary: the human being's ability to grow and change. Called the High Holy Days, Rosh Hashanah and Yom Kippur are a time for deep thought, self-examination, and prayer, all of which are hard to do.

Rosh Hashanah, which means Head of the Year, celebrates the beginning of the world and the creation of man and woman. It also marks the start of the Jewish year, the first of Tishri, which coincides with September or early October, a time when summer vacations have ended, school has started again, and in many places, the weather has turned crisp and cool. New classes, new clothes, and new activities distinguish the season.

The Jewish New Year is not like the New Year's holiday celebrated on January 1. Instead of throwing parties and using noisemakers, Jews celebrate joyfully but quietly. They look back at the past year to decide which deeds felt right and which deeds did not. Because God is everywhere, even within each human being, self-examination is a way of searching for God.

There is no sudden revelation of having found something. The search takes time. It doesn't even begin on Rosh Hashanah. It begins in Elul, the month before Tishri. This is a month of preparation, but unlike other holidays that require cooking, cleaning, or building, the preparation is invisible because it takes place within.

Rosh Hashanah is also called Yom Teru'ah, Day of the Shofar. A shofar is a ram's horn, a three-thousand-year-old musical instrument that is blown in the synagogue during the Rosh Hashanah service (if the holiday doesn't fall on the Sabbath). One of the laws of the holiday is to hear the high-pitched blasts of the shofar. Its urgent sound seems to say, "Wake up! Think! What did you do last year? What will you do this year?"

The shofar also expresses feelings that cannot be put into words: feelings of wanting to change and being excited by the chance to do so, but also of being afraid of changing. Like a baby's cry that proclaims new life, the shofar may be the cry of the new self that is born on Rosh Hashanah.

The ten days between Rosh Hashanah and Yom Kippur are called the Days of Awe. These are tender and delicate days, when people look at the year that has passed and face up to their mistakes, errors in judgment, or wrongdoings. This is called *teshuvah*, which means return. If you've made a mistake, you can do something to correct it. First you think of what you've done. The next step is to apologize. The last step answers the question "How do I know that I've done *teshuvah*, that I've really changed?" The answer is that you don't make the

The Jewish Calendar

The Jewish calendar is different from the Gregorian, or Christian, calendar used in most countries. Rather than follow the earth's 365-day journey around the sun as the Gregorian calendar does, the Jewish calendar follows the moon's cycle. Each month begins with a new moon and ends twenty-nine and a half days later, with the waning of the moon. The problem with this system is that a year, or twelve lunar cycles, is only 354 days, so every few years an extra month is added, around March, to keep pace with the sun. Otherwise, the holidays would fall at different times of the year. Imagine Hanukkah in July!

Following the sun or the moon is not the only difference between the calendars. The Gregorian calendar has been counting for just under two thousand years. The Jewish calendar begins counting years from the time of Creation, roughly six thousand years ago.

same mistake again. Only after you've completed these steps can you ask forgiveness of God.

Teshuvah is part of how people change. The other ingredients are *tefillah*, which means prayer, and *tzedakah*, which means justice, or giving to those in need. On every Sabbath and holiday, even the poorest Jew must set aside something for someone with less.

Beginning is the key word for the High Holy Days, and the climax to beginning again is Yom Kippur, the last day of the High Holy Days. Although it is usually translated as the Day of Atonement, Yom Kippur literally means the Day of Cleansing. Jews do not eat, work, or go to school on Yom Kippur. The day is spent studying and praying in the synagogue. Some Jews don't wear leather shoes or belts, to show respect for animals and to express the hope that one day no life will be taken by another.

There is a feast in the late afternoon just before the eve of Yom Kippur because the holiday, despite its seriousness, is joyful. It is a day to be at peace with God and oneself. The hallah, or bread, at this meal is sometimes shaped like a ladder to help one's prayers ascend to heaven.

After this meal, no food or drink is consumed until after sunset the next day. This is a twenty-five-hour fast. Children under thirteen and sick adults don't have to fast, but starting at about nine years of age, some children begin to fast by skipping breakfast or waiting until two o'clock to eat lunch. Fasting is not a punishment. It is a reminder of how dependent people are upon God and upon one another for food. The fast is also a reminder of how it feels to be hungry, and that the poor need help.

Kol Nidre, a service at the synagogue, follows the meal. The service begins when the setting sun is level with the treetops. The atmosphere of the synagogue on this night is extraordinary. First of all, more people attend this service than any other during the year. Everywhere you look you see the color white, symbolizing freshness and simplicity. The rabbi and cantor wear white, the holy ark holding the Torah (scrolls containing the Five Books of Moses) has been changed to white, and all the Torahs have white coverings instead of their usual brightly colored ones. Even the flowers decorating the synagogue are white.

Carrying Torahs, the rabbi, cantor, and a few members of the congregation circle around the room. Everyone stands near where the Torahs pass, to reach out and touch them with a corner of their prayer shawls or prayer books. This is like greeting a friend with a handshake or a kiss. When the Torahs have been returned to the ark, the chanting of the Kol Nidre begins. The prayer haunts, touches, and moves Jews, and like the shofar, it opens the heart. The Kol Nidre, which means All Vows, is chanted three times, clearing the slate between each person and God: all promises that could not be kept during the year are now forgotten. It is time to start again.

Many people stay in the synagogue all day on Yom Kippur. At five o'clock the Ne'ilah service, which means Closing the Gates, begins. The holy ark is left open for the service, and those who are able stand until the end of the holiday, which comes at approximately seven o'clock, when the first three stars appear in the sky.

The service closes with the holiest Jewish prayer, the Shema: "Hear, O Israel, the Lord our God, the Lord is One." Shema means "hear." Some holidays have symbols that you can see, such as the Hanukkah menorah, or taste, such as the Passover matzah. But on the High Holy Days, people listen. They listen to the shofar, the Kol Nidre, others asking their forgiveness, and themselves. And God listens, too.

Moses's Mistake

There is no Hebrew equivalent for the word sin. *The closest is* het, *which means "missing the mark." Just as we are not able to hit a bull's-eye every time, we may have trouble mastering our feelings, especially anger, in every situation. In Judaism, no one is expected to be perfect, just better. The way we change is by seeing our mistake, admitting the mistake, and not doing it again. Everyone does* teshuvah, *even Moses, because all human beings make mistakes.*

Moses climbed to the top of Mount Sinai to receive God's second most important gift, the Ten Commandments. The first gift was life, but life was no treasure by itself. So God gave Moses a set of rules, the Ten Commandments, to help people know how to live their lives. Made for all time, the rules were hammered into a huge stone slab, five commandments on each side.

Despite the stone's weight, Moses ran down the mountain, eager to show the Israelites their great gift. He imagined everyone waiting anxiously for his return, but when he reached the bottom of the mountain, no one was waiting for him.

The Israelites hadn't believed that he would return. They hadn't even believed that he would see God. So they had decided to make their own god. They had melted their jewelry into a little gold calf, and when Moses found them, they were praying to it.

Everything about Moses was great, including his temper. Trembling with rage, he thrust the heavy stone that God had given him over his head and flung it to the ground. The Ten Commandments broke into more pieces than there are stars in the sky.

God ordered Moses into a cave for forty days to make a new stone tablet. When Moses finished his work, he was tired but calm. "Good," God said. "Now put the new stone tablet into a special chest."

After Moses carefully placed the Ten Commandments in the holy ark, he heard God's voice again. "Be sure to put in the broken pieces, too, Moses. Set them beside the whole stone."

Moses looked at the beautiful new Ten Commandments and then winced at the rubble of the first tablet. "Every time I see this mess, I remember how I lost my temper."

"Exactly!" God replied. "And that's why the broken pieces, your mistake, are holy, too."

Maybe Even Higher

Study and prayer alone are not holy. It's what they move you to do that's holy. The importance of the deed is illustrated in the following tale adapted from a story by the Yiddish writer I. L. Peretz.

Once long ago, in a village where everyone was poor but hopeful, there lived a wise and holy man named Zuzya. Whenever anyone had a worry, the first thing they did was to talk to Zuzya.

Each morning the month before the New Year, the entire village awakened before dawn to say special prayers together. Every person added a few private ones: "Dear God, please let me make enough money to feed my family!" "Please make my mother well!" "Please send my children wonderful marriage partners!" "Stop my neighbor from stealing my chickens!" When the villagers prayed, they were glad Zuzya was there to hear them.

One morning Zuzya was late for praying. The prayer room felt empty without him. "Where could he be?" everyone asked one another. He was nowhere to be seen — not in the prayer house, not in the study house, and not in his own house. The door to his little home stood wide open. Of course, no one would think of stealing from Zuzya.

The villagers agreed that Zuzya could be only in one place — heaven! Every citizen of the town, from the youngest child to the oldest grandmother, needed help. Who else but Zuzya could go to God and ask for help?

Everyone believed this except for one man who was new to the village. He studied day and night, night and day, with his nose nearly touching his book. Behind his back, the villagers called him Stick, because he was dry and lifeless. When he heard Zuzya had gone to heaven to plead for the people, the stranger smiled for the first time in his life. In fact, he fell down laughing at the idea of Zuzya having a chat with God. When he finally stopped laughing, he shrugged and said, "How can you people be so ignorant? Besides, who cares where Zuzya goes in the morning?"

But really, the stranger was curious. Late that night, after evening prayers, he crept into Zuzya's house and crawled under his bed. Zuzya was so absorbed in a conversation with God that he didn't hear the man enter the house. The stranger planned to stay awake the whole night to see where Zuzya went during early morning prayers.

Somebody else might have fallen asleep, but not a man accustomed to studying day and night, night and day. He read all night under the bed, until he heard a long sigh and a groan over his head. Zuzya had been awake for a while, thinking about the troubles of the people, and his heart hurt for their suffering.

Somebody else might have wept at the sound of Zuzya's sadness, but not the stranger. He was full of learning, not compassion. So he lay there, waiting, without understanding Zuzya's groans.

It was still dark when Zuzya got up. As the springs of the bed whined, the stranger shivered. Here he was, with the holiest and wisest man in the village, at the holiest time of the day. He began to sweat. His skin became bumpy with goose pimples, but he was a disciplined man. He clenched his jaw to keep his teeth from chattering and didn't budge.

Zuzya went to his closet and took out a bundle. He untied it and pulled out huge boots; baggy, rough pants; a short, clumsy jacket; a big fur hat and a long, broad leather belt studded with brass nail heads. When he put on the clothes, he no longer looked like Zuzya. He looked like a peasant who lived in the forest. From one of the pockets a piece of string dangled. The stranger held his breath as Zuzya knelt beside the bed and pulled out an axe from underneath the mattress.

Securing the axe in his belt, Zuzya left the house. The stranger, shaking and sweating, followed.

Zuzya walked quickly along the dark streets, with the moon shining on him between houses. The stranger, close behind him, listened to his thumping heart keep time to Zuzya's clumping boots.

Zuzya headed for the woods right outside the town, and when he had walked thirty steps, he stopped in front of a young tree. The stranger's mouth dropped open as he saw Zuzya pull the axe from his belt and take a mighty swing at the tree. Two whacks brought it down with a splintery thud. Zuzya quickly lopped off the branches and cut the sapling into kindling. He tied the pieces into a bundle with the string in his pocket, lifted the wood onto his shoulder, poked the axe back into his belt, and turned back toward the village.

Walking down a side street in the poorest neighborhood, he stopped by a tumbledown shack and knocked on a rag-stuffed window.

"Who's there?" asked a weak, frightened voice.

"I!" answered Zuzya roughly, disguising his voice to sound like a woodsman.

"Who's I?" asked the voice within the house.

And Zuzya answered, "Vassil," a common peasant name.

"Who do you want, Vassil?"

"I have wood to sell, very cheap," said the make-believe Vassil. And without waiting for permission, he walked into the house.

The stranger crept up to the door and peered in. In the gray light of early morning, he saw a few pieces of broken furniture. In the lopsided bed lay an old woman covered with rags. She struggled to raise her head and said bitterly, "Wood? You expect a poor widow to buy wood? With what?"

"I'll trust you for the money," said the pretend Vassil. "It's only six pennies."

"And how will I ever get six pennies to pay you back?" she whimpered.

"Don't be foolish!" Zuzya said sharply. "You are a poor, sick, old widow, yet I am willing to trust you with a little wood — I'm sure you'll pay me back. Yet you don't trust God, the compassionate Source of Life, to give you six miserable cents?"

"And who will light the fire for me?" the old woman groaned. "Have I strength even to lift my head?"

"I'll light the stove for you," Zuzya answered.

As Zuzya set the fire, he sang the morning prayers. By the time he said the last prayer, the fire was blazing.

What the stranger witnessed through a crack in the door taught him more than all his books and years of study. From that day on, when Zuzya spoke, the stranger listened.

Years later, whenever one of the people in the village told their children of the time Zuzya flew straight up to heaven, the stranger never laughed. He only nodded and said softly, "Maybe even higher."

The Shofar

The shofar, a trumpet made from a ram's horn, once heralded great events. It summoned armies to battle, proclaimed a new king, and announced the Sabbath and festivals. If you have one, you can blow it on Shabbat, on birthdays, or when anything important is about to happen.

The word *shofar* comes from a root word meaning "hollow" in Hebrew. The shofar is an empty instrument that becomes special only with a person's breath in it. It takes a human being to make it holy.

The person chosen to blow the shofar for the High Holidays is called the *ba'al teki'ah*, the master of the shofar. Being a *ba'al teki'ah* is a great honor, and it takes practice, because it's not easy to blow a shofar. Three different kinds of sounds are made with the shofar. One is *shevarim*, three short blasts, which sound like sobs. Another is *teru'ah*, nine very fast short notes, like wailing. *Teki'ah* is a long, clear, mellow tone. *Teki'ah gedolah*, "the great blast," is supposed to be as long as the shofar blower can manage. When the time comes for the shofar to be blown, everyone pays close, even anxious, attention. The *ba'al teki'ah* is blowing for the entire congregation, and if there is a mistake, it is shared by all who listen.

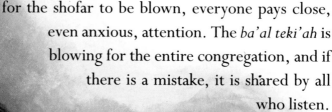

New Year Cards

About five hundred years ago, German Jews began the custom of wishing one another a good new year. Soon Jews throughout Europe were expressing this wish in writing. Today we send new year cards to help us keep in touch with friends and relatives who live far away.

Make an envelope by folding a square piece of paper along the dotted lines as shown in the drawing.

Pressed flowers can then be used to make beautiful and unusual cards. Flat flowers such as pansies, honeysuckle, or even dandelions are the easiest to use. Most of these flowers will still be blooming in late August, which is when you should start making the cards. Lay the flowers, along with a few leaves from the plant, between waxed paper, and put them in a heavy book such as a telephone book.

Place several heavy books on top of the phone book, and leave them like this for two weeks. Gently remove the flowers from the book. They should be flat and dry, and their colors should still be vivid. With a watercolor brush, paint the backs of the flowers with white glue. Then arrange the flowers on the front of a folded sheet of paper, and press lightly. After the glue is dry — in a couple of hours — open the card and write your message in Hebrew: *"Shanah Tovah"*

or in English: "May your year be good and sweet."

Honey Cake

The food for Rosh Hashanah is perfect for anyone with a sweet tooth, because the custom is to serve nothing sour or bitter for the season. The hope is that sweetness will last for the whole year. This cake is a traditional Rosh Hashanah treat.

4 eggs
1 cup sugar
1 cup honey
¾ cup coffee
½ cup melted margarine
4 cups sifted unbleached
   white flour
3 teaspoons baking powder
1½ teaspoons baking soda
¼ teaspoon ground cloves
¼ teaspoon ground nutmeg
¼ teaspoon ground
   cinnamon
¼ cup chopped walnuts
¼ cup seedless raisins
½ teaspoon almond extract
whipping cream
dash cinnamon
dash sugar

Preheat the oven to 350°F. Grease a 10 x 10–inch or 14 x 10–inch baking pan.

In a large bowl, cream the eggs and sugar; beat until light and fluffy. In a small bowl, combine the honey and coffee. Add the margarine to the egg mixture, then stir in the honey and coffee. Sift the flour again, into a large bowl, adding the baking powder, baking soda, and spices; add the nuts and raisins. Combine the dry ingredients and the liquid mixture, and beat until completely blended and smooth. Add the almond extract.

Pour the batter into the prepared pan, and bake for one hour. Whip the cream, sprinkling in the cinnamon and sugar. Cut the cake into squares and serve with the whipped cream topping.

Hallah

Hallah is a long, oval braided bread prepared for Shabbat and festivals. The hallah made on Rosh Hashanah can be formed into a shape resembling a crown, since Rosh Hashanah is the "head" of the year. The Rosh Hashanah hallah can also be formed into a little ladder, on which prayers travel up to God.

Prepare the hallah dough following the instructions on page 173, and let it rise for at least two hours. It should be twice as big as it was when you first put it in the bowl. Preheat the oven to 350°F. Punch the dough down, then put it on a lightly floured cutting board. Shape it into a long snake, about eighteen inches long. Place the dough on a cookie sheet. To make a crown-shaped hallah, hold one end in place and wrap the rest of the dough in a circle around it, so that the center is higher than the outer circle. It should be round and turbanlike when you're done. Separate the white of an egg from the yolk, saving the yolk. Dip your fingers into the yolk and smear it over the dough. This will make the crust shiny after the hallah has baked. Sprinkle sesame seeds on top.

You make a ladder hallah with a long snake of dough, too. Break it into thirds and put one piece aside. Take the other two pieces and lay them parallel to one another, about six inches apart. Break the third piece into three pieces and lay them across the first two pieces of hallah like the rungs of a ladder. Glaze the ladder with egg yolk as you did for the crown hallah.

Bake the crown hallah for 45 minutes, the ladder hallah for 35 minutes. Take the cookie sheet out of the oven, lift the bread off, and tap the bottom of the bread. If it sounds hollow, it's done. After a blessing, the hallah is dipped in honey and eaten.

I'm Sorry

by Myra Cohn Livingston

The ten days between Rosh Hashanah and Yom Kippur are a time to forgive and to ask forgiveness from friends and family. To forgive is hard, but to ask forgiveness may be even harder.

> *To try to say it,*
> *To put it into words,*
> *To make it come out of my mouth happens slowly.*
>
> ### *THERE*
>
> *I have said it.*
> *Only one small say:*
> *But it is said.*

How to Bring the Messiah

The rabbis of long ago said that eating on the day *before* Yom Kippur is as holy an act as fasting is *on* Yom Kippur. Jewish festivals alternate fast and feast days because no one knows whether fasting or feasting will bring the Messiah sooner. So people do both.

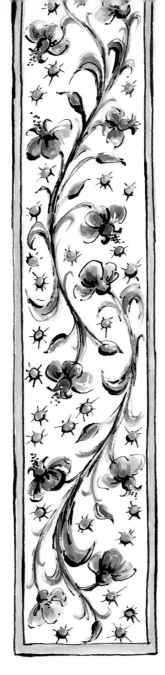

Jonah and the Great Fish

by Clyde Robert Bulla

The following adventure is read from the Torah on Yom Kippur afternoon. Jonah's story is a reminder that no one escapes God, since no one can escape himself or herself. The story also celebrates the ability to grow from one's mistakes and God's forgiveness. Human beings may change, and even a prophet like Jonah cannot predict his future.

LONG AGO IN THE LAND OF ISRAEL there lived a man named Jonah. He had a farm with a house, a field, and a garden. He had a small donkey to pull his plow.

One day after work he sat down in his garden to rest.

While he rested, he went to sleep. A voice wakened him. It was a voice like wind and rain and thunder.

"Arise!" it said. "Arise and go to Nineveh, that great city. Go and preach to the people against their wickedness!"

Jonah fell forward into the dust. He was trembling with fear, for he knew he had heard the voice of the Lord.

He lay in the dust. The voice did not speak again. He lifted his head.

He said to himself, "The Lord has spoken, and I must obey."

The Lord had said, "Arise!"

Jonah got to his feet.

But the Lord had said, "Arise and go to Nineveh."

Jonah asked himself, "Why must I go there?"

Nineveh was far away in the land of Assyria. The people of Assyria were enemies of Israel. It was true that they were wicked, but what was their wickedness to him?

He thought on these things, and his heart grew stubborn. He said in his heart, "Why should I preach to my enemies? I will not go."

Yet he knew the Lord would come again. The Lord would say, "You have not obeyed me. My punishment shall fall upon your head."

Jonah went into his house. He closed the door. "I will not go to Nineveh!" he said. "Neither will I stay to be punished by the Lord!"

He waited until night came. He went outside. He climbed upon his donkey and rode away.

All night he rode. As the sun came up, he fell in with a band of traders riding camels.

The traders were friendly. Jonah rode with them by day. He camped with them by night. They rode together until they came to Joppa, a city by the sea.

Jonah was far from home. Still he feared that even here the Lord might find him.

A ship was ready to sail from the harbor.

Jonah said to the captain, "Take me with you."

"Do you have money?" asked the captain.

Jonah went to the marketplace. There he sold his donkey for a handful of silver. He took the money back to the ship. He paid his fare and went on board.

The ship sailed. The sky was clear. The sailors were happy, and they sang.

But as the ship sailed beyond the harbor, the sky grew dark. A storm swept the sea.

The ship carried a cargo of grain. The sailors threw the cargo overboard to lighten the ship so that it would not sink.

The sailors believed in many different gods. Each man prayed to his god, "Save us! Save us!"

Jonah was weary from his journey to Joppa. He had gone down into the ship and was fast asleep.

The captain went to him. He shook Jonah and said, "Arise, you sleeper. Pray to your God to save us."

On deck the sailors shouted to be heard above the wind.

"Someone on this ship has brought the storm upon us," said one.

"Let us cast lots," said another. "This will tell us who has brought the storm."

A sailor came with the lots. Each lot was a small square of wood with a number on it. He put them into the cup.

Two sailors stretched a cloth tightly between them. Each man in turn shook the cup so that only one lot fell out onto the cloth. Everyone watched to see who would shake out the lot with the low number.

The last of the sailors shook a lot from the cup.

"The low number has not fallen," said the men. "None of us has brought the storm."

Jonah and the captain came on deck.

"Will you cast with us?" asked the sailors.

The captain shook out one of the lots.

The men read the number on the lot. "It is not our captain who has brought the storm," they said.

A sailor held out the cup to Jonah.

Jonah drew back.

"You must cast with us," said the sailor.

Jonah took the cup. He shook it until one of the lots fell.

The men read the number on the lot. It was the low number.

"He has brought the storm!" they said. "It is Jonah! It is Jonah!"

They looked into his face. "Who are your people?" they asked. "What is your country?"

"I am a Hebrew from the land of Israel," he answered, "and I fear the Lord, the God of Heaven."

Now he knew that even here the Lord had found him. He knew that nowhere on land or sea could he hide from the Lord.

The sailors asked him, "What shall we do to be saved?"

"Take me up and throw me into the sea," said Jonah. "Then the waters shall be calm, for the storm was sent because of me."

But no one wished to lay hands on Jonah.

The sky grew darker. The waves rose above the sides of the ship.

The sailors prayed to the Lord, "Let us not all be lost because of one man!"

Their voices could not be heard above the roar of the storm.

They waited no longer. They laid hands on Jonah and threw him into the sea.

At once the sky began to clear. The wind became a breeze, and the ship sailed in calm waters.

The sailors thanked God, even while they thought of Jonah. "He is lost," they said, "that we might be saved."

But Jonah was not lost. The Lord had caused a great fish to rise near the ship. As the waves closed over Jonah, the fish had swallowed him.

Jonah was alive inside the fish. He lived in terrible darkness, and he cried out to the Lord.

Three days and three nights passed. Then the Lord spoke to the fish. The fish opened its great mouth and cast Jonah out upon dry land.

Jonah felt the earth beneath him. He saw the sky and the sun, and he breathed the clean air. He gave thanks to the Lord.

Again the voice of the Lord spoke to him. "Arise," it said, "and go to Nineveh!"

This time Jonah obeyed.

He came to the gates of the city.

"Let me pass," he said, and the soldiers and guards made way for him.

Within the city he preached the words the Lord had given him: "After forty days Nineveh shall be destroyed!"

The people listened and were afraid.

The king himself came down from his throne. He dressed in rough sack-cloth and sat in ashes. This was a sign that he had put aside his wicked ways. It was a sign that he believed in the word of God.

The other people of Nineveh dressed in sackcloth and rubbed themselves with ashes. They prayed to the Lord.

The Lord heard their prayers, and He forgave them. After forty days the city was not destroyed.

The people were joyful. They feasted together. They danced in the streets.

But Jonah was not joyful.

He had obeyed the Lord. He had preached to the people of Nineveh. Still he

said to himself, "They are my enemies." He had not wished them to be saved, and he was angry because the Lord had not destroyed their city.

He went away into the desert nearby.

There he sat, in a poor shelter he had made of sticks. He looked toward Nineveh. He hoped that the Lord might yet destroy the city.

The Lord watched over Jonah. He sent a plant to grow beside the shelter.

In a single day the plant grew tall. It put forth branches and leaves. Its shade kept the burning sun from Jonah, and he was pleased.

That night he lay in the shadow of the plant. He saw the moon through its branches. He heard the whispering sound of the leaves. He began to love the plant as he would have loved a friend.

In the morning he looked into the branches, and he cried out. The leaves were dying.

"I must find water," he said.

But he quickly saw that water could not save the plant. Already the leaves had turned brown. The branches had drooped.

"Must you die? Must you die so soon?" said Jonah, and he wept.

The plant fell in a small, dry heap. An ugly worm crawled out of the stalk.

Jonah took up a stick. He tried to strike the worm, but it disappeared into the ground.

"Lord," he said, "You sent the worm to kill my plant. It was You, O Lord!"

Once more the sun beat down on Jonah's head. A burning wind began to blow.

He could not bear the heat of the wind and sun, and he said, "It is better for me to die than to live!"

The Lord spoke. "Is it well for you to be angry because of the plant?"

"Yes," said Jonah. "It is well for me to be angry."

The Lord said, "You have felt pity for something that grew and died in a day and a night. Is not the city far greater than the plant? Shall I not feel pity for Nineveh with its many thousands of people?"

Then Jonah was ashamed of his anger. He understood that the Lord loved all people, whether they be of Israel or Assyria or any other land. He bowed his head and thanked the Lord for His mercy.

From Fast to Feast!

A long, steady note on the shofar signals the end of Yom Kippur. But it is really another beginning — of a new year, a renewed self, a new moon. The new moon of Tishri is blessed outdoors before the fast is broken. Then everyone joins together in a light meal. After the meal, many families go outside and hammer in the first post for the sukkah, the handmade shack in which they will celebrate Sukkot five days later. This connects the end of Yom Kippur, a serious, fasting holiday, to the beginning of Sukkot, a happy, bountiful holiday.

Sukkot

Sukkot

The Great Day

Sukkot is the longest and happiest holiday season of the Jewish year. The eight-day harvest festival, beginning on the fifteenth of Tishri, is celebrated in a sukkah, a richly decorated little house built just for Sukkot.

When you step into the sukkah, it is like going back to a time when people lived close to the earth and seasons were an intimate part of life. For people today, Sukkot is a yearly opportunity to camp out and to remember that human beings are part of the natural world.

Three thousand years ago, the Jews were slaves in Egypt. After four hundred years of this slavery, God instructed Moses to lead the Jews out of Egypt to a land they'd only heard about. Many were afraid to leave; even though their lives were harsh and bitter, at least they knew what to expect. On their journey with Moses, they had their doubts about whether they had made a mistake. They didn't go from slavery to a life of ease right away. They wandered in the wilderness without trees to protect them from the desert sun. Many worried that they wouldn't survive, but God sheltered them with seven clouds. One was under their feet, one was over their heads, four formed walls, and the last cloud led the way.

After forty years in the desert, the Jews finally reached the land God had promised. They became farmers and grew olives, wheat, and grapes. When it came time for the harvest in the early fall, the farmers needed to be near the crops to pick them quickly in case of a sudden storm. They built little wooden huts in the fields and lived in them until they had finished harvesting.

In time, Sukkot became a celebration of both the forty-year wandering and the harvest. The sukkah became a symbol of protection and peace, and the holiday became a time of feasting and of thanking God for the harvest. In

Israel twenty-five hundred years ago, it was the grandest holiday of all. Simply called He-Hag, the Holiday, it was the one time of year when farmers relaxed — they had harvested their crops, and it was too soon to plant for the following year.

If Sukkot sounds like Thanksgiving, it may be no coincidence. After the Pilgrims survived their first year in America, they wanted to celebrate. Some historians think that because the Pilgrims knew about Sukkot from the Bible, they modeled the first Thanksgiving feast after it. Like the Jews, the Pilgrims were grateful not only for the food that they had grown but also for God's protection in their new land. The first Thanksgiving celebration fell in October and lasted for three days.

Four Species

Four special plants are as important to Sukkot as the sukkah. In Hebrew these plants are called *arb'ah minim*, the four species. Each is different from the other, and each has its own meaning.

The *lulav* is a tall green palm branch. It was the national emblem of ancient Israel. Its upright shape represents righteousness. Three sprigs of *hadasim*, shiny myrtle leaves, are tied to the right side of the *lulav*, and two sprigs of *aravot*, delicate willow, are tied to the left. Some people believe that the myrtle is the plant Adam and Eve took from the Garden of Eden. It is a reminder of the world to come. The willow, which grows by streams, is a reminder of life-giving water. The fourth plant, the *etrog*, or citron, looks like a large, lumpy lemon. This ancient fruit may have been the fruit of knowledge in the Garden of Eden.

Two thousand years ago, the rabbis compared the fragrances and tastes of the plants and said that the *arb'ah minim* also stand for types of human behavior. The *lulav* has no fragrance, but because it is the leaf of the palm tree that bears dates, it does have taste. The myrtle branches have no taste but have a wonderful fragrance. The willow has neither taste nor fragrance. Finally, the *etrog* possesses both fragrance and taste. In this way, the *lulav* is like the person who is learned but doesn't do good deeds; the myrtle is like the person who is ignorant but kind to others; the willow is like the person who is neither learned nor does good deeds; and the *etrog* is like the person who is both learned and kind. These four belong together because the world needs all kinds of people.

On Sukkot, people hold the four species together and say a special blessing over them in the sukkah or in the synagogue.

30

A Whole Heart

The four plants can also represent the body. The lulav *stands for the backbone, or strength; the myrtle for the eyes, or enlightenment; the willow for the lips, or prayer; and the* etrog *for the heart, or understanding. The heart is the most important part to bring to a holiday, because it completes the prayer. A heart must be whole to perform a good deed; a mitzvah cannot be done halfheartedly.*

Two men of Helm, a village famous for its outrageously stupid people, could not afford separately to buy a *lulav* and an *etrog*. So they went into partnership and bought them together, but this soon proved to be an unsatisfactory solution, for they immediately began to argue about who would have the honor of making the first blessing.

The rabbi, the only wise person in Helm, overheard them. "Stop fighting," he said. "I'll settle this." Taking a knife in his hand, he quickly cut the *etrog* right down the middle and handed each man a half. Both men were horrified. The *etrog* was worthless now, because it must be whole to fulfill the mitzvah, or commandment, of Sukkot.

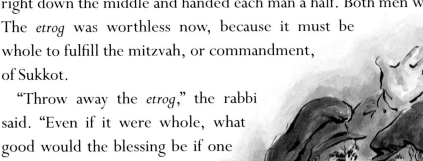

"Throw away the *etrog*," the rabbi said. "Even if it were whole, what good would the blessing be if one of you were angry and jealous of the other? The most perfect *etrog* in the world is nothing compared to the blessing that comes from a whole heart."

Invisible Guests

During Sukkot, it's especially important to invite the poor to eat in the sukkah, because the poor reflect the image of God. The people you invite into the sukkah will eat the food prepared not for them but for the ushpizin, *invisible guests "who see but who are not seen." These guests are the fathers and mothers of the Jewish people: Abraham, Isaac, Jacob, Joseph, Moses, Aaron, and David; Sarah, Rebecca, Rachel, Leah, Miriam, Hannah, and Deborah. The following Hasidic tale illustrates the importance of hospitality.*

Shlomo was a learned man who was often asked for advice on matters ranging from how to prepare foods properly to how to settle an argument. But instead of being pleased that he was so respected, Shlomo resented the many interruptions by people needing him. They kept him from his studies, which he believed were far more important than people's questions.

One day a woman came to Shlomo's study holding a chicken. "Has it been killed properly?" she asked.

"Out of here!" Shlomo shouted. Alone in his room, he prayed that he be left alone to pursue his work. No one came to see him, and he was happy.

When the High Holy Days came, Shlomo fasted and prayed harder than anyone. Right after Yom Kippur, he asked some of his neighbors to help him build a sukkah. In his village, the custom was for people to build sukkot together. But since God had granted Shlomo's prayer to be left alone, no one helped him.

"Very well," he said, "I'll build it myself." So he got out some wood and nails and built his sukkah. The first night he entered his sukkah alone, because he had not invited anyone. Of course, he did invite Abraham and Sarah to enter.

But they wouldn't come in. "We can't come into a sukkah where no one else is welcome," they said. At once Shlomo realized that rituals and prayers are meaningless unless you understand their lesson. Shlomo had missed the whole point of Sukkot. He asked God to revoke his prayer, and he welcomed neighbors to his house.

House on the Roof

A Sukkot Story

by David Adler

ONE DAY, the old man from apartment 3D dragged a heavy wood crate up the front steps of his building.

"Don't scratch the paint with that junk," the owner of the building yelled. "I don't have the halls painted so you can scratch the paint right off."

The next day, the old man collected acorns and autumn leaves. When he brought them into the building, the owner yelled from her window, "Don't drop anything. If someone falls and gets hurt, I'll be the one to pay."

For more than a week, inside his small apartment, the old man hammered and sewed and polished.

He collected old magazines, and the owner yelled, "Junk and more junk. Most people throw it out. You collect it." The old man collected more crates . . . old clothes . . . empty bottles . . . and broken branches. He brought everything into the building. Each time he walked up the front steps, the owner yelled.

Then, one evening, just before sunset, the old man left the building. He was wearing his suit and derby hat. The owner sat by her window and watched.

About an hour later, he returned. He was talking and laughing. His grandchildren were with him. They were talking and laughing, too. They followed the old man up the front steps and into the building.

The owner followed them. They walked up three flights of stairs, past the old man's apartment, and onto the roof.

In the corner, there was a small hut. The walls were made of wood crates. The roof was made of broken branches.

Inside was a small table covered with a patchwork cloth. The cloth was made from torn clothes. Candles burned in candlesticks. The candlesticks were made of old bottles. Chains of acorns and autumn leaves hung from the roof. On the walls were pictures cut from old magazines. On the table there was wine, soda, cake, and cookies.

"Wow!" "Beautiful," the children said. "This is the most beautiful sukkah." The old man smiled.

The old man drank wine. The children drank soda and a little wine. They all ate cake and cookies.

A few days later, the owner of the building brought the old man to court. "It's my building and my roof," she told the judge.

"Well," the judge asked the old man, "what do you have to say?"

"Your Honor," the old man answered, "thousands of years ago, my people were slaves in Egypt. When they escaped to the desert, they had no time to build homes. As they traveled, they built temporary huts. Each autumn, we celebrate the holiday of Sukkot by building and living in huts just like theirs. That's what I did. Now in only four days the holiday will be over. I would like so much to keep my sukkah for just that long."

The judge thought and thought. Then he turned to the owner. "You're right," he said to her. "It is your building. No one should be allowed to build on your roof without your permission."

Then the judge said to the old man, "I'll give you just ten days to take your sukkah down." The judge smiled.

"Ten days," the old man thought. Then he smiled, too.

The Sukkah

It is necessary for you to rejoice within the sukkah and to show a cheerful countenance to guests. It is forbidden to harbor thoughts of gloom, and how much more so feelings of anger within the sukkah, the symbol of joy.   *Zohar*

A sukkah is a reminder of the shelter God made for the Israelites in the wilderness and of the farmers' harvest shacks in ancient Israel. But remembering history is not the only reason to build a sukkah; there are other more immediate meanings.

The sukkah is only a temporary place, like a sand castle. The wind blows through the sukkah, and rain drips through its leafy roof. Some people think they can control everything in their lives, but the sukkah reminds us that no house can protect us from all of life's dangers: everyone is vulnerable to the forces of nature.

It may be fun to eat meals in or to camp out in a sukkah for a week, but would you want to stay in one permanently? Poverty forces some people to live in shacks all the time. Unless you have experienced this for yourself, you cannot know how uncomfortable and difficult it can be. Just as the sukkah is not a closed building, so people must not close themselves off from the suffering of other people.

The sukkah is also a reminder that a simple life is best. Thousands of years after the wilderness experience, the Jewish people realized that the years of wandering had had much good in them. Despite the harshness, it was a pure time, when everyone lived in the same way with enough, but not more than enough.

Wild plants and animals are stronger than cultivated species because they survive with little help from the environment. People can grow strong in a harsh place, too. Spending a week in a sukkah is not as harsh as a real pioneering experience, but the contrast between the simple sukkah and a comfortable house may make you wonder if you really need all the appliances and gadgets in your life. Maybe you'd feel stronger with fewer of them.

Just because a sukkah is temporary and frail doesn't mean it can't be a splendid creation. It is, after all, a symbol of God's protection. There are, however, a few rules. A tree or second story can't be above the sukkah, because the stars need to twinkle through the leafy roof covering. The roof must be made from plants cut from their roots. The sukkah must be no less than five feet high and no more than thirty feet high.

One last rule: the sukkah must be rebuilt every year. You can't leave it up for the next Sukkot. This is because you hope that next year will be the time when all the world will sit together in one sukkah peacefully, and no one will need to build separate sukkot.

Building a Sukkah

You'll need the following materials to build an eight-by-eight-foot freestanding sukkah that is cozy but large enough for an eight-day family picnic:

4 pieces of 2-by-4 lumber, cut into 8-foot lengths

16 pieces of 1-by-4 lumber, cut into 8-foot lengths

"common" nails (the kind with heads that can be pulled out easily with a claw hammer when you dismantle the sukkah later)

hammer

ladder

Use industrial-grade wood or number 3 pine. Lay out the materials, and include an adult in the building crew.

To make your first wall, lay two of the two-by-fours on the ground, and nail four one-by-fours between them as shown in the picture. Be sure the lumber is flat side up. Build a second wall in the same way, and set it aside. Take four more one-by-fours, and hammer them to points A, B, C, and D of

the first wall to form a right angle. (This is easier to do if the wall is on the ground.) When you've finished hammering the one-by-fours, you should have completed two sides of the sukkah.

Bring the wall that you set aside earlier over to the unattached ends of the one-by-fours, and hammer them together at right angles to make a third wall. This is simple if one person holds the frame and another person hammers. Now you should have a freestanding sukkah without its *sekhakh*, or roof.

Take the last four one-by-fours and nail them across the top. These boards will support the tree branches. Any branch with leaves on it will do: Pine, palm, and olive branches are possibilities. Even corn stalks make a good *sekhakh*.

Old sheets, blankets, and bamboo fencing are the easiest materials for completing the walls. Staple any of these coverings tightly to the inside of the frame so they won't flap in the wind. You'll need enough materials for

three sides of the sukkah. (When you take down the sukkah, use a staple remover so that you won't harm the sheets or blankets.) The fourth wall can be left open, especially in a warm climate. But if you want to close it off, just staple another sheet to that side, leaving one edge of the sheet free so that you can get in and out. If you're lucky enough to have some old doors and windows around, they make wonderful walls for the sukkah, too.

The floor is not important, but if you have an old piece of carpet, it makes the sukkah fancier. Some people lay sand on the floor to remind them of the desert wandering.

The sukkah is now ready to decorate. It is traditional to decorate the sukkah with real or handmade fruits, but you can also hang other objects or draw pictures on the walls. If you plan to use the same sheets every year, draw pictures right on them with permanent-color marking pens. Lean branches and corn stalks against the walls to give a feeling of autumn. To show the link between the High Holy Days and Sukkot, hang New Year's cards and posters of the *ushpizin*, the invisible guests who are invited to visit the sukkah. The posters can be found in Jewish bookstores, or, if you feel inspired, you can draw your own pictures of the invisible guests. Don't forget the most important adornment of all: the sign that says *Baruh ha-ba*, which means "Blessed be the one who comes" or "Welcome" in Hebrew. Here's how it looks in Hebrew:

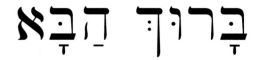

Stuffed Pumpkin

Sukkot is a perfect time to have a party, since the focus of the holiday is on harvesting food crops and being hospitable. Besides, a sukkah makes a naturally merry setting for a party. Here is a recipe to help you celebrate the fall harvest.

1 pumpkin
salt
nuts
raisins
chocolate chips

Preheat the oven to 350°F. Cut a circle, six inches in diameter, in the top of a pumpkin. (Since you need a sharp knife and a fair amount of muscle to do this, make sure an adult is around to help.) Lift the "lid" off and, with a spoon, remove all the pulp and seeds from the inside into a large bowl. Set aside the pumpkin.

With your fingers, separate the seeds from the pulp, putting the seeds into a colander and the pulp into a second large bowl. Wash the seeds in the colander until they are free of remaining pulp. Spread them on a cookie sheet covered with aluminum foil. Lightly salt the seeds with kosher (coarse) salt or plain salt. Roast the seeds for 15 minutes.

While the seeds are roasting, line the inside of the pumpkin with aluminum foil. When the seeds are cool, mix them with nuts, raisins, and chocolate chips, and put the mixture into the pumpkin. Set this in the sukkah for munching.

Simhat Torah

Rejoicing in the Torah

The last day of the High Holidays season, Simhat Torah, the Rejoicing of the Torah, is the most exuberant celebration of the year. The Torah is made up of the Five Books of Moses. *Torah* also means all learning. Anyone who thinks that devotion to the Torah is always solemn and serious would be astounded at Simhat Torah. It is a buoyant celebration in honor of a book that has been read and reread for three thousand years and still has new things to say.

In the synagogue, the "book" is a handwritten double scroll. By reading a section each week, it takes a year to complete the whole Torah. On Simhat Torah, which falls on the twenty-third of Tishri, the last portion is read. The joy comes not only from finishing the book, but also from the pleasure of knowing that you're about to begin it again. Every time you read the Torah, it's different. As you grow, you find new meanings in the words.

On the eve of Simhat Torah, the synagogue is noisy. Disorder is the order of the day! Children come to synagogue with brightly colored flags topped with apples, which symbolize the harvest. This is one time when parents don't insist that children sit quietly in their seats and listen to the rabbi. Instead, they are encouraged to march around the synagogue when all the Torahs are taken out of the holy ark.

The last story in the Torah tells of the forty-year wandering. As soon as this portion is read, the first book of the Torah, Genesis, is read. There is no pause between the reading of the last and first portions, because the study of the Torah never ends.

A Flag for Simhat Torah

Here is a quick and easy way to make your own flag to carry in the Torah parade in the synagogue. You can use the flag of Israel or make your own design. The Star of David is not the only Jewish symbol. In fact, it wasn't used until five hundred years ago. You can use Sukkot symbols, but be sure to include the most important Simhat Torah symbol: the Torah. Take a piece of white 9 x 12–inch fabric. Cut your designs from a piece of colored fabric, and glue them to the white piece with white glue. Staple the flag to an 18-inch-long thin round stick. (Most hardware stores carry them.) Be sure to leave enough room at the top for the apple.

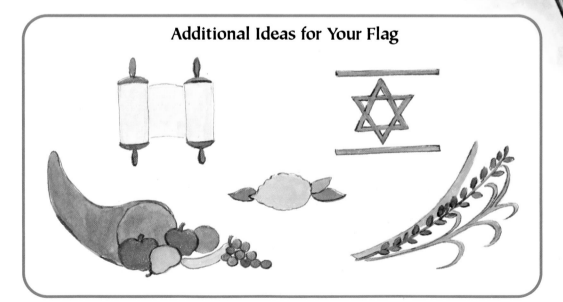

Additional Ideas for Your Flag

Hanukkah

Hanukkah

Eight Nights, Eight Lights

Hanukkah is a holiday of opposites. On the one hand, the winter holiday is a delight — eight days of songs, games, candlelight, gifts, and delicious foods. Yet Hanukkah recalls a violent story about the first great war for religious freedom.

Twenty-four hundred years ago, the Jewish people lived as farmers, shepherds, and grape growers in Israel. They believed one invisible god had created the entire world and had given them laws to follow for a good and just life. Other peoples at that time worshiped gods of nature, whose power and presence could be sensed by everyone. They could feel the warmth of the sun god and praise the rain god for thundershowers. To them, every element of the world represented a god.

The idea of just one invisible god puzzled many peoples, especially the worldly and sophisticated Greeks. They valued education, physical beauty, and celebrations, and worshiped a family of gods who were supposed to have special powers over their lives and activities.

Many Jews liked the Greek way of life. Their language, clothes, and beliefs spread around the world. Some Jews left their farms to take up trade with the Greeks. Returning home with money, new customs, and perhaps a new Greek name such as Jason instead of Joshua, they became the trendsetters of the Jewish community. Still, not everyone followed the new fashion; a few Jews spoke out against the new life-style.

Antiochus IV, the Syrian king who came to power in 175 B.C.E., insisted that all Jews become Greek. When Jews didn't convert quickly enough, Antiochus banned their holidays, burned their books, and killed anyone, including mothers and children, who wouldn't bow to Zeus, the chief Greek god.

Antiochus erected altars to Zeus everywhere, including in the Great Temple in Jerusalem. In those days, there was only one Jewish temple in the world; it was meant to be the most beautiful building ever, because it was dedicated to God. It was made of fragrant cedar and polished granite. On Passover, Shavuot, and Sukkot, Jews came from all over Israel to celebrate at the Temple. They brought gifts from the harvest of their farms to the Temple to thank God for their crops.

In 167 B.C.E., Syrian soldiers came to the mountain village of Modin, in Israel, to meet with Mattathias, an elderly and respected Jewish priest. With flattery and bribery, they tried to coax him and his five sons to come to an altar where they had erected a statue of Zeus. They also wanted Mattathias to kill a pig and eat some of it, a food forbidden to Jews: he would set an example for other Jews to follow. Mattathias refused.

Suddenly a villager, tempted by the soldiers' promises of riches, stepped in front of the altar, ready to bow before it. Enraged at the traitor, Mattathias struck and killed him and a soldier. Tearing down the altar, he thundered,

"Whoever is for God, follow me!" Then he and his sons, along with a few followers, fled to the mountains and planned their attack on Antiochus.

Mattathias and his sons — called the Maccabees, which means "hammers" — led a small group of soldiers against Antiochus's immense army. The Maccabees, fighting with sticks and stones and farm tools, won victory after victory against the Syrians, who were armed with swords and javelins and used elephants as tanks.

How the Maccabees won is a mystery and a miracle. It helped that they knew the country better than the Syrians. And they knew they had to win, because if they didn't, the Jewish people would be destroyed. But mostly, they won because they felt the spirit of God inside them, and that gave them special strength.

On the twenty-fifth of Kislev, 165 B.C.E., the Maccabees returned triumphantly to Jerusalem, ready to celebrate. Instead, they grieved. The Temple was filthy — blood, dirt, and ashes covered everything. All the books, Torahs, and candlesticks were gone.

Worst of all, there was only a drop of oil left for the menorah. Made of gold, the menorah was a lamp with seven branches, one for each day of the week. It was supposed to burn continuously. One drop of oil would last for only one day. But when the oil was poured into the lamp, it burned for a second day, and a third. In all, it burned for eight days, and that is why Hanukkah is eight days long. Hanukkah means Feast of Dedication, because the Maccabees rededicated, or restored, the Temple to what it was supposed to be, a holy place in which to celebrate great days.

The story of Hanukkah is not about military victory, but about miracles, especially the miracle of a few people triumphing over tremendous odds in a struggle for the right to practice their religious beliefs. This is not a magical or supernatural miracle, but something inside everyone, the spirit to choose what a person believes is right, no matter how hard or dangerous that may be.

Judith the Warrior

This story comes from the Book of Judith, which is a book in the Apocrypha, a collection of Jewish writings written between 200 B.C.E. and 200 C.E.

Wind and rain stung the young woman's face. Clammy mud clung to her feet, but Judith paid no attention. "Judah! Where are you?" she screamed above the wind. She had spent the day climbing the hills of Israel searching for her cousin, Judah Maccabee.

A weary voice responded, "Over here." Judith followed the sound into a cave and found Judah huddled by a sputtering fire, trying to get warm. His eyes were guarded as he looked up at his beautiful cousin. "Don't ask me again," he warned.

Judah Maccabee had been fighting Antiochus, the Syrian king, and his immense army for almost three years. Even though Judah's soldiers were farmers and ridiculously outnumbered, they were brave and battled with all their might.

Judah needed all the help he could get, but one volunteer he turned away again and again. "No, Judith," he said, "you cannot join our army. Fighting is a man's job."

Judith sighed. She had heard all this before. "I know, I know. If I want to help, I should join the camp as a cook for the soldiers," she said, mimicking Judah's deep, gravelly voice. "I'm already doing that, but I want to do more than cook!" she exclaimed. "Look at you! You're worn out. You need me!"

Judah shook his head. The conversation was over. Judith gathered up her soggy skirts and stormed out of the cave.

Before she reached the lowlands, she knew what she would do. She would be a soldier, and food would be her weapon. Holofernes, the Syrian general in charge of all the soldiers, adored Judith, even though she always refused to look at him. But now she decided it was time to pay him a visit.

She packed a large basket of food and went to visit the general in the hills above her village. When she reached the camp, the guards stopped her until Holofernes appeared. "Judith," he said, grinning broadly, "what a surprise! Come into my tent."

Judith smiled her sweetest smile and followed him. Waving his hand at the lavish banquet of meats and fruits in his tent, Holofernes invited Judith to eat. "No, thank you, Holofernes. You know my people can only eat food prepared in a special way," she answered. "I've brought this for both of us," and she opened her basket of cheeses, olives, and wine.

"Oh, I love Jewish food!" Holofernes told her and bit into a wedge of salty cheese. After a few minutes he said, "Let me have some of that wine. The cheese and olives are making me thirsty."

Judith smiled her sweetest smile and poured him a huge goblet of wine. Holofernes beamed. As soon as he drained the cup, she refilled it. Over and over she kept his glass full. After a while his eyelids became heavy. His head nodded as he struggled to keep his eyes from closing, but soon he fell backward, snoring loudly.

Judith didn't waste a second. She leaned over him, unsheathed his knife from his belt, and whacked off his head. She stuffed the head into her basket and ducked out of the tent, all the while smiling her sweetest smile at the guards outside.

First she returned to her village, where she proudly displayed Holofernes's head to her family and friends. They wept and cheered at her bravery. They begged her to stay so they could prepare a feast in her honor, but she said no.

"I can't stay right now," she told them. "I have to visit my cousin Judah. I have something to show him," she said, patting her basket.

Cheese and dairy foods are traditional parts of the Hanukkah celebration, but most people don't know why. If you tell them this story, don't do it while they're eating latkes *and sour cream!*

The Menorah

The Hanukkah menorah, or candle holder, is called a *hanukkiyah*. It has eight places for a separate flame — the flames must not touch — and a ninth place for an extra flame called the *shammash*, or "servant" candle, which lights the others.

A menorah can be made of anything that won't burn — clay, a potato, even a baseball bat! The only rule is that the *shammash* be higher, lower, or farther away from the other candles. For almost two thousand years, the menorah has inspired extraordinary designs. The most popular design resembles a tree with eight branches. As a tree, the menorah combines earthly strength with heavenly light.

Here are a few ideas for making your own *hanukkiyah*: a distributor cap from an eight-cylinder car; a Noah's ark with clay animals; and a hammer with nine holes drilled in the handle, to pun on the meaning of Maccabee.

Lights

The *hanukkiyah* is lit at nightfall, when it is late enough for the candles to bring light to a darkened room but early enough for everyone in the family, including the babies, to see the ceremony. On the first night, a candle is placed at the far right end of the menorah, perhaps because Hebrew is read from right to left. Each night another candle is added to the left of the preceding candle. That way each candle has its own night. The *shammash* is lit first, and it is used to ignite the other candles one by one every night, starting with the newest candle and moving toward the right. Then the lit *shammash* is placed in the middle branch or holder of the menorah. The candles should burn for at least half an hour, and on Friday night they should be lit before the Shabbat candles. During the eight nights, everyone should get to light the candles at least once, because the miracle was for all of us.

The candlelight is not to be used for work. The beautiful light is only to proclaim the miracle. Altogether, forty-four candles burn during Hanukkah, and these small, pretty candles are a reminder that even the small, when they stand together, can light the darkness.

Hanukkah takes place during the darkest time of the year. Just as the menorah grows brighter each day of Hanukkah, so the sun increases its light each day of winter until the days are long again. During the winter, Hanukkah is a light that warms and cheers us.

There are Jewish prayers for nearly everything — for different foods, for the first flower of the season, for new clothes, even for earthquakes — so it is only natural that there is a blessing for one of God's holiest gifts, light. As soon as the *shammash* is lit, two blessings are said. The first is a blessing over the Hanukkah candles:

You abound in blessings, Source of Light, Our God, Ruler of All Worlds, who has made us holy with Your commandments, and has commanded us to kindle the light of Hanukkah.

Baruh atah adonai, eloheinu meleh ha-olam, asher kidushanu b'mitzvotav vitzivanu l'hadlik ner shel hanukkah.

The second blessing gives thanks for the miracles:

You abound in blessings, Source of All, Our God, Ruler of the Universe, who performed miracles for our ancestors in those days, at this time.

Baruh atah adonai, eloheinu meleh ha-olam, she-asah nissim lavotanu ba-yamim hahem bazman hazeh.

On the first night, a third prayer is added to give thanks for being able to celebrate the holiday. This prayer is also said at the beginning of most holidays and at new and happy events:

You abound in blessings, Source of All, Ruler of the Universe, who keeps us alive and in good health so that we can be here to celebrate this festive day.

Baruh atah adonai, eloheinu meleh ha-olam, shehehiyanu ve-kiymanu vehigianu lazman hazeh.

Zlateh the Goat

by Isaac Bashevis Singer

AT HANUKKAH TIME the road from the village to the town is usually covered with snow, but this year the winter had been a mild one. Hanukkah had almost come, yet little snow had fallen. The sun shone most of the time. The peasants complained that because of the dry weather there would be a poor harvest of winter grain. New grass sprouted, and the peasants sent their cattle out to pasture.

For Reuven the furrier it was a bad year, and after long hesitation he decided to sell Zlateh the goat. She was old and gave little milk. Feyvel the town butcher had offered eight gulden for her. Such a sum would buy Hanukkah candles, potatoes and oil for pancakes, gifts for the children, and other holiday necessaries for the house. Reuven told his oldest boy, Aaron, to take the goat to town.

Aaron understood what taking the goat to Feyvel meant, but he had to obey his father. Leah, his mother, wiped the tears from her eyes when she heard the news. Aaron's younger sisters, Anna and Miriam, cried loudly. Aaron put on his quilted jacket and a cap with earmuffs, bound a rope around Zlateh's neck, and took along two slices of bread with cheese to eat on the road. Aaron was supposed to deliver the goat by evening, spend the night at the butcher's, and return the next day with the money.

While the family said good-bye to the goat, and Aaron placed the rope around her neck, Zlateh stood as patiently and good-naturedly as ever. She licked Reuven's hand. She shook her small white beard. Zlateh trusted human beings. She knew that they always fed her and never did her any harm.

When Aaron brought her out on the road to town, she seemed somewhat astonished. She'd never been led in that direction before. She looked back at him questioningly, as if to say, "Where are you taking me?" But after a while she seemed to come to the conclusion that a goat shouldn't ask questions. Still, the road was different. They passed new fields, pastures, and huts with thatched roofs. Here and there a dog barked and came running after them, but Aaron chased it away with his stick.

The sun was shining when Aaron left the village. Suddenly the weather changed. A large black cloud with a bluish center appeared in the east and spread itself rapidly over the sky. A cold wind blew in with it. The crows flew low, croaking. At first it looked as if it would rain, but instead it began to hail as in summer. It was early in the day, but it became dark as dusk. After a while the hail turned to snow.

In his twelve years Aaron had seen all kinds of weather, but he had never experienced a snow like this one. It was so dense it shut out the light of the day. In a short time their path was completely covered. The wind became as cold as ice. The road to town was narrow and winding. Aaron no longer knew where he was. He could not see through the snow. The cold soon penetrated his quilted jacket.

At first Zlateh didn't seem to mind the change in weather. She too was twelve years old and knew what winter meant. But when her legs sank deeper and deeper into the snow, she began to turn her head and look at Aaron in wonderment. Her mild eyes seemed to ask, "Why are we out in such a storm?" Aaron hoped that a peasant would come along with his cart, but no one passed by.

The snow grew thicker, falling to the ground in large, whirling flakes. Beneath it Aaron's boots touched the softness of a plowed field. He realized that he was no longer on the road. He had gone astray. He could no longer figure out which was east or west, which way was the village, the town. The wind whistled, howled, whirled the snow about in eddies. It looked as if white imps were playing tag on the fields. A white dust rose above the ground. Zlateh stopped. She could walk no longer. Stubbornly she anchored her cleft hooves in the earth and bleated as if pleading to be taken home. Icicles hung from her white beard, and her horns were glazed with frost.

Aaron did not want to admit the danger, but he knew just the same that if they did not find shelter they would freeze to death. This was no ordinary storm. It was a mighty blizzard. The snowfall had reached his knees. His hands were numb, and he could no longer feel his toes. He choked when he breathed. His nose felt like wood, and he rubbed it with snow. Zlateh's bleating began to sound like crying. Those humans in whom she had so much confidence had dragged her into a trap. Aaron began to pray to God for himself and for the innocent animal.

Suddenly he made out the shape of a hill. He wondered what it could be. Who had piled snow into such a huge heap? He moved toward it, dragging Zlateh after him. When he came near it, he realized that it was a large haystack which the snow had blanketed.

Aaron realized immediately that they were saved. With great effort he dug his way through the snow. He was a village boy and knew what to do. When he reached the hay, he hollowed out a nest for himself and the goat. No matter how cold it may be outside, in the hay it is always warm. And hay was food for Zlateh. The moment she smelled it she became contented and began to eat. Outside the snow continued to fall. It quickly covered the passageway Aaron had dug. But a boy and an animal need to breathe, and there was hardly any air in their hideout. Aaron bore a kind of a window through the hay and snow and carefully kept the passage clear.

Zlateh, having eaten her fill, sat down on her hind legs and seemed to have regained her confidence in man. Aaron ate his two slices of bread and cheese, but after the difficult journey he was still hungry. He looked at Zlateh and noticed her udders were full. He lay down next to her, placing himself so that when he milked her he could squirt the milk into his mouth. It was rich and sweet. Zlateh was not accustomed to being milked that way, but she did not resist. On the contrary, she seemed eager to reward Aaron for bringing her to a shelter whose very walls, floor, and ceiling were made of food.

Through the window Aaron could catch a glimpse of the chaos outside. The wind carried before it whole drifts of snow. It was completely dark, and he did not know whether night had already come or whether it was the darkness of the storm. Thank God that in the hay it was not cold. The dried hay, grass, and field flowers exuded the warmth of the summer sun. Zlateh ate frequently; she nibbled from above, below, from the left and right. Her body gave forth an animal warmth, and Aaron cuddled up to her. He had always loved Zlateh, but now she was like a sister. He was alone, cut off from his family, and wanted to talk. He began to talk to Zlateh. "Zlateh, what do you think about what has happened to us?" he asked.

"Maaaa," Zlateh answered.

"If we hadn't found this stack of hay, we would both be frozen stiff by now," Aaron said.

"Maaaa," was the goat's reply.

"If the snow keeps on falling like this, we may have to stay here for days," Aaron explained.

"Maaaa," Zlateh bleated.

"What does 'Maaaa' mean?" Aaron asked. "You'd better speak up clearly."

"Maaaa. Maaaa," Zlateh tried.

"Well, let it be 'Maaaa' then," Aaron said patiently. "You can't speak, but I know you understand. I need you and you need me. Isn't that right?"

"Maaaa."

Aaron became sleepy. He made a pillow out of some hay, leaned his head on it, and dozed off. Zlateh too fell asleep.

When Aaron opened his eyes, he didn't know whether it was morning or night. The snow had blocked up his window. He tried to clear it, but when he had bored through to the length of his arm, he still hadn't reached the outside. Luckily he had his stick with him and was able to break through to the open air. It was still dark outside. The snow continued to fall and the wind wailed, first with one voice and then with many. Sometimes it had the sound of devilish laughter. Zlateh too awoke, and when Aaron greeted her, she answered, "Maaaa." Yes, Zlateh's language consisted of only one word, but it meant many things. Now she was saying, "We must accept all that God gives us — heat, cold, hunger, satisfaction, light, and darkness."

Aaron had awakened hungry. He had eaten up his food, but Zlateh had plenty of milk.

For three days Aaron and Zlateh stayed in the haystack. Aaron had always loved Zlateh, but in these three days he loved her more and more. She fed him with her milk and helped him keep warm. She comforted him with her patience. He told her many stories, and she always cocked her ears and listened. When he patted her, she licked his hand and his face. Then she said, "Maaaa," and he knew it meant, I love you too.

The snow fell for three days, though after the first day it was not as thick and the wind quieted down. Sometimes Aaron felt that there could never have been a summer, that the snow had always fallen, ever since he could remember. He, Aaron, never had a father or mother or sisters. He was a snow child, born of the snow, and so was Zlateh. It was so quiet in the hay that his ears rang in the stillness. Aaron and Zlateh slept all night and a good part of the day. As for Aaron's dreams, they were all about warm weather. He dreamed of green fields, trees covered with blossoms, clear brooks, and singing birds. By the third night the snow had stopped, but Aaron did not dare to find his way home in the darkness. The sky became clear and the moon shone, casting silvery nets on the snow. Aaron dug his way out and looked at the world. It was all white, quiet, dreaming dreams of heavenly splendor. The stars were large and close. The moon swam in the sky as in a sea.

On the morning of the fourth day Aaron heard the ringing of sleigh bells. The haystack was not far from the road. The peasant who drove the sleigh pointed out the way to him — not to the town and Feyvel the butcher, but home to the village. Aaron had decided in the haystack that he would never part with Zlateh.

Aaron's family and their neighbors had searched for the boy and the goat but had found no trace of them during the storm. They feared they were lost. Aaron's mother and sisters cried for him; his father remained silent and gloomy. Suddenly one of the neighbors came running to their house with the news that Aaron and Zlateh were coming up the road.

There was great joy in the family. Aaron told them how he had found the stack of hay and how Zlateh had fed him with her milk. Aaron's sisters kissed and hugged Zlateh and gave her a special treat of chopped carrots and potato peels, which Zlateh gobbled up hungrily.

Nobody ever again thought of selling Zlateh, and now that the cold weather had finally set in, the villagers needed the services of Reuven the furrier once more. When Hanukkah came, Aaron's mother was able to fry pancakes every evening, and Zlateh got her portion too. Even though Zlateh had her own pen, she often came to the kitchen, knocking on the door with her horns to indicate that she was ready to visit, and she was always admitted. In the evening Aaron, Miriam, and Anna played dreidel. Zlateh sat near the stove watching the children and the flickering of the Hanukkah candles.

Once in a while Aaron would ask her, "Zlateh, do you remember the three days we spent together?"

And Zlateh would scratch her neck with a horn, shake her white bearded head and come out with the single sound which expressed all her thoughts, and all her love.

Hanukkah Games

The rabbis set the laws for Hanukkah, but the people made the holiday sweet and fun. They couldn't work by the light of the Hanukkah candles, so they spent the candlelit hours playing games.

Dreidel, the most popular Hanukkah game, began when Antiochus forbade the Jews to study Torah, the Jewish Bible. Groups of children who had secretly memorized the entire Torah studied together until they heard the footsteps of the Syrian soldiers approaching. Then they quickly pulled out spinning tops and pretended to be playing games.

In the Middle Ages, dreidel playing became more complicated as rules were borrowed from a German gambling game played with a four-sided top with a different letter on each side. The Jewish version used the letters

נ (*nun*),

ג (*gimel*),

ה (*he*), and

ש (*shin*),

which stand for *Nes gadol hayah sham* ("A great miracle happened there"). Although the rabbis disapproved of gambling, they accepted the dreidel because of this Hanukkah message.

They also discovered another religious connection. Each Hebrew letter has a numerical equivalent, and the four letters on the dreidel add up to 358, the same number as the letters of the word *Messiah*. The Messiah will show the way for future miracles.

Here's how you play. Everyone starts with a pile of whatever you're gambling for — raisins, nuts, pennies, or Gummy Bears. Take five raisins, say, from the pile in front of you and put them into the main pile. Each player takes a turn spinning the dreidel and seeing what letter lands on top. This is what the letters mean:

- נ   *Nun*:   Do nothing.
- ג   *Gimel*:   Take the main pile.
- ה   *He*:   Take half the main pile.
- ש   *Shin*:   Give half of your pile.

Players who have nothing left to give are out of the game, and the player who outlasts the others is the winner.

Dreidel can also be played just as a spinning game. Whoever spins the dreidel the longest is the winner. The spin of the dreidel is like the world. Everything happens in cycles. As the earth spins on its axis, the seasons change, and so do the fortunes of people. The mighty Antiochus fell when the small army of Maccabees overturned his rule.

Besides dreidel games, you can play ordinary games such as cards and dominoes, turning them into special Hanukkah games. The opposing pieces in chess and checkers can become the Maccabees battling the Syrians. Scrabble becomes Hanukkah Scrabble when you give fifty bonus points for words related to Hanukkah, such as *candle, light,* and *miracle.*

You can have a treasure hunt for Hanukkah *gelt,* or money, hidden around the house and keep the treasure you find. Speaking of hiding, even hide-and-seek can become a game of Maccabees hiding from the Syrian army in the hills and caves of Israel.

Latkes

Sometimes when you remember a special time, you can almost smell your memory. A whiff of popcorn might remind you of the movies, or a roasting turkey might remind you of Thanksgiving at your grandparents' house. Hanukkah smells like latkes, small potato pancakes. Fried in oil, latkes are a reminder of the tiny jug of oil that miraculously lasted for eight days.

3 large potatoes
1 small onion
2 beaten eggs
2 tablespoons flour
1 teaspoon salt
pinch of pepper
½ cup of vegetable oil

Before you begin cooking, it's a good idea to have an adult around. Frying with oil is a tricky business.

Wash the potatoes very well, but you don't have to peel them — they're healthier and easier to prepare unpeeled. Grate them coarsely into a bowl. Grate in the onion. (You can use a food processor for this if you have one.) Add the beaten eggs, flour, salt, and pepper. Let the mixture sit for ten minutes to thicken. Pour off the excess liquid.

Heat the vegetable oil for one minute in a frying pan. Gently drop the potato mixture into the pan, making each circle two inches across. When the *latkes* are brown around the edges, turn and fry them until the other sides are crispy. Drain them on paper towels and eat them with sour cream and/or applesauce. (Caviar is good, too!) Makes about 24 pancakes.

Maoz Tzur
(Rock of Ages)

Liturgy
Eng. verse: M. Jastrow, G. Gottheil

Traditional

Moderately

Ma - oz tzur y' - shu - a - ti l'ha na - e l' - sha - be - ah,
Rock of a - ges, let our song praise Thy sav - ing pow - er;

Ti - kon bet t' - fi - la - ti, v'sham to - da n'za - be - ah.
Thou, a - midst the rag - ing foes, wast our shel - t'ring_ tow - er.

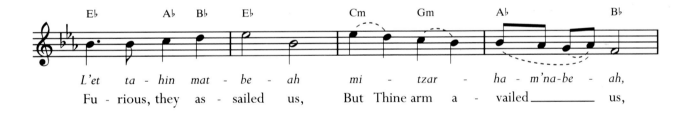

L'et ta - hin mat - be - ah mi - tzar - ha - m'na-be - ah,
Fu - rious, they as - sailed us, But Thine arm a - vailed_____ us,

Az eg - mor b' - shir miz-mor, ha - nu - kat ha - miz - be - ah.
And Thy word_ broke their sword_ When our own strength failed_ us.

Tu B'Sh'vat

Tu B'Sh'vat

The Trees' Birthday

Tu B'Sh'vat, the New Year of the Trees, is one of the few Jewish holidays that isn't connected to a historical event. But a holiday can do more than honor the past — it can also celebrate our hopes. Tu B'Sh'vat celebrates our hope and intention to make the world more green and healthy. As we learn more about how important it is to take care of the natural world so that nature can take care of us, maybe Tu B'Sh'vat will become as popular as Passover and Hanukkah.

Tu B'Sh'vat, which means the fifteenth of Shevat, falls in the middle of the month of Shevat, under a full moon in midwinter. The ancient farmers believed that on that day the sap begins to rise in the fruit trees in Israel and the land starts to awaken from winter. In the Gregorian calendar, the holiday falls between the end of January and the middle of February.

This is a holiday to be celebrated not at home or in the synagogue, but outdoors, where trees live. It's a time to eat fruit, plant new trees and to notice how much trees, giant, quiet and still, bring beauty, nourishment, and shelter to our lives.

In Israel Tu B'Sh'vat has special meaning. When Jews returned to Israel to resettle the land one hundred years ago, the country was mostly swamp and desert, with very few trees. The Jewish National Fund began to build forests in Israel by encouraging Jews from all over the world to "plant" trees; really, Jews contributed a small sum of money to have a tree planted in their name in Israel.

By planting a tree in Israel, Jews living far away could feel that they were part of the land. Millions of saplings were planted, and now there are over 165 million trees in Israel. Sometimes, when people who planted trees visit Israel for the first time, they want to find their tree!

Some Jewish families follow the ancient custom of planting a cedar tree when a boy is born and a cypress when a girl is born. The trees are planted on Tu B'Sh'vat. When children grow up and get married, the branches from their trees are cut to make a marriage canopy.

Five hundred years ago in Israel, the Cabalists, a group of people who searched for holiness in everything, created a seder, a dinner with special foods and a ceremony, for Tu B'Sh'vat to celebrate the connection of all living things to the earth. As in the Passover seder, the number four is important, because it represents the four seasons, the four elements that the world is made of, and the four corners of the earth. With blessings, special fruit, and wine, the seder is divided into four parts.

The seder is celebrated at nightfall with lots of candles, flowers, and fragrant greens. Because life begins in the darkness of the womb, the first part of the seder begins with readings about earth and winter. In this section, we eat fruit that is hard on the outside and soft on the inside, such as a pomegranate, walnut, or coconut. We drink white wine because white is the color of snowy winter.

The second section celebrates water and the awakening of spring. The food for this part is soft outside and hard inside, such as a cherry, an olive, or an avocado. A little red wine is mixed with the white for the second blessing over the wine.

The third section concentrates on air and summer. The fruit eaten is soft throughout, such as berries, figs, and grapes. Now the wine is more red than white, because red is both hot and strong. The earth is awakening.

The fourth and final part celebrates fire and autumn. Now the earth is fully awake. We drink pure red wine, which represents the spark inside each of us that connects us to God.

Some people try to eat at least fifteen different kinds of fruit to celebrate Tu B'Sh'vat. Certain fruits have special meanings related to events or sayings in the Bible. The apple represents God because of the apple tree in the Garden of Eden. Nuts represent the Jewish people, because they can be hard, medium, or soft, like the three different characteristics of people. Figs represent peace, and the carob, which tastes a little bit like chocolate, represents humility because it is the food of the poor.

Honi and the Carob Tree

Adapted from the Midrash

Honi was a man of great power who prayed with all his heart. He had only one fault. He said anything that popped into his head, and sometimes he regretted it.

One day he was taking a walk in his neighborhood in Jerusalem. There he saw an old man digging in the earth. Because he was ancient, the man dug slowly, taking up just a little earth with each scoop of the shovel.

"What are you doing, grandfather?" Honi called to the man.

Without stopping, the old man answered, "I am planting a carob tree."

Honi burst out laughing. "How crazy, old man! To spend how little time you have left doing that! You won't live long enough to eat of the fruit of that tree. Nor will you ever sit under its shade."

"True, young man," answered the tree planter, "but trees are beautiful things to have. My children will eat the fruit, and my grandchildren will enjoy the shade. I ate the fruit from trees my father planted, and I sat under the shade from trees my grandfather planted. Now I will prepare for those who come after me."

Honi shook his head. "If I were you, I'd plant a fast-growing tree, like an olive tree or a fig, so you might live to eat its fruit and get something for your hard work." The old man smiled and went on digging. Honi yawned. It was warm in the middle of the day, and suddenly he felt so sleepy that he could barely move. Shoving aside a few small rocks, he lay down where he stood and stretched out to sleep.

He dreamed the rocks around him grew bigger and bigger until they hid him from view. When he awoke, it was morning. "Oh, I must have slept here all night," he thought. He began to get up and found his body stiff and creaky.

Finally he tottered to his feet. He looked at his hands, then at his clothes. He shivered with fear. His clothes were in shreds, and his cheeks and chin were hidden by a long, white beard.

"I'm old!" he exclaimed out loud. "How long have I slept?" he wondered. He looked around and found himself in the middle of a fruit orchard. A tall, full carob tree heavy with sweet pods hung low. Honi picked one and hungrily

chewed it, savoring its rich taste. Just then a little boy passed by. "Stop!" Honi shouted to the boy. "Who are you?"

"I am Moshe ben Shimon Halevi," the boy replied.

"No! Moshe ben Shimon Halevi!" repeated Honi. "Why, he is an old man!"

"You must mean my great-grandfather," the boy said, chewing a carob pod. "He died many years ago. I was named for him. This is the tree he planted in the last years of his life. About seventy years ago."

Seventy years! Honi had slept a long time, but at last he understood the old man's wisdom.

A Sample Seder

Here are a few readings and blessings that celebrate nature. They can be appreciated anytime, but are especially appropriate for a Tu B'Sh'vat seder.

Earth

And God said:
Let the earth put forth grass herb yielding seed
And fruit trees bearing fruit after its own kind
Wherein is the seed thereof upon the earth.

Genesis 1:11

It is forbidden to live in a town which has no garden or greenery.   *Kiddushin 4:12*

i thank You God for most this amazing
day: for the leaping greenly spirits of trees
and a blue true dream of sky; and for everything
which is natural which is infinite which is yes

e. e. cummings

Two men were fighting over a piece of land. Each claimed ownership and bolstered his claim with apparent proof. To resolve the dispute, they went to the rabbi. The rabbi listened but couldn't come to a decision — they each seemed to be right. Finally he said, "Since I cannot decide to whom this land belongs, let us ask the land." He put his ear to the ground, and after a moment straightened up. "Gentlemen, the land says that it belongs to neither of you — but that you belong to it."   *Talmud*

Water

The Mole thought his happiness was complete when, as he meandered aimlessly along, suddenly he stood by the edge of a full-fed river. Never in his life had he seen a river before — this sleek, sinuous, full-bodied animal, chasing and chuckling, gripping things with a gurgle and leaving them with a laugh, to fling itself on fresh playmates that shook themselves free, and were caught and held again. All was a-shake and a-shiver — glints and gleams and sparkles, rustle and swirl, chatter, and bubble. The Mole was bewitched, entranced, fascinated. By the side of the river he trotted as one trots, when very small, by the side of a man who holds one spellbound by exciting stories; and when tired at last, he sat on the bank, while the river still chattered on to him, a babbling procession of the best stories in the world, sent from the heart of the earth to be told at last to the insatiable sea.

Kenneth Grahame
The Wind in the Willows

Air

And God said, "Let there be light." And there was light.   *Genesis 1:3*

Every part of the vegetable world
is singing a song
and bringing forth a secret
of the divine mystery
of the creation.
    Rav Kook

Then the Lord God formed the human of the dust of the ground, and breathed into the nostrils the breath of life; and the human became a living soul.   *Genesis 11:7*

Fire

When you walk across the fields with your mind pure and holy, then from all the stones, and all growing things, and all animals, the sparks of their souls come out and cling to you, and then they are purified and become a holy fire in you.   *Hasidic saying*

Master of the Universe
Grant me the ability to be alone;
May it be my custom to go outdoors each day
Among the trees and grasses,
Among all growing things
And there may I be alone,
And enter into prayer
To talk with the one
That I belong to.
    Rabbi Nachman of Bratslav

A Tree Is Nice

by Janice May Udry

TREES ARE VERY NICE. They fill up the sky. They go beside the rivers and down the valleys. They live up on the hills. Trees make the woods. They make everything beautiful.

Even if you have just one tree, it is nice too.

A tree is nice because it has leaves. The leaves whisper in the breeze all summer long. In the fall, the leaves come down and we play in them. We walk in the leaves and roll in the leaves. We build playhouses out of the leaves. Then we pile them up with our rakes and have a bonfire.

A tree is nice because it has a trunk and limbs. We can climb the tree and see over all the yards. We can sit on a limb and think about things. Or play pirate ship up in the tree.

If it is an apple tree, we can climb it to pick apples.

Cats get away from dogs by going up the tree. Birds build nests and live there. Sticks come off the tree too. We draw in the sand with the sticks.

A tree is nice to hang a swing in. Or a basket of flowers. It is a good place to lean your hoe while you rest.

A tree is nice because it makes shade. The cows lie down in the shade when it is hot. People have picnics there too. And the baby takes his nap in his buggy in the shade.

A tree is nice for a house to be near. The tree shades the house and keeps it cool. The tree holds off the wind and keeps the wind from blowing the roof off the house sometimes.

A tree is nice to plant. You dig the biggest hole you can and put the little

tree in. Then you pour in lots of water and then dirt. You hang the shovel back in the garage. Every day for years and *years* you watch the little tree grow. You say to people, "I planted that tree."

They wish *they* had one, so they go home and plant a tree too.

Plant a Tree

According to Rabbi Yohanan ben Zakkai, if you know the Messiah is coming and you're in the middle of planting a tree, you should first finish planting and then go greet the Messiah. That's how important trees are. So, plant a tree!

You can buy a seedling from a nursery. Look for one that is in a container no larger than one gallon. The bigger the tree, the more fragile it is to plant. Dig a hole twice the depth and width of the container. Fill the hole with water. When the water has been absorbed, fill the tree's container with water. When the water drains, gently tap the container so that the soil comes out whole in the shape of the container, as though you were making a sand castle. This is the root ball.

Loosen a few roots from the bottom and put the root ball in the hole. Fill the hole in with soil so that the tree is upright and there is a little well around the base to catch water. Water the ground around the tree immediately after planting and every day for a week. Watering twice a week will be enough after that. By late spring, the tree will have new growth, or if you planted a fruit tree without leaves, it will begin to sprout its leaves.

These are good instructions for planting a Tu B'Sh'vat tree in, say, Israel or California, but if you live in a colder place, such as New York, the ground will still be frozen on Tu B'Sh'vat. You can't dig a hole in winter. But you can still plant a tree. Go to your local nursery and ask for tree seeds. Plant the seeds in a flowerpot, put it on a window sill that gets lots of sun, water it every day, and watch the seeds sprout. In spring, when the snow is gone, you can plant your seedling outdoors, following the instructions given above.

The Tu B'Sh'vat Song

Brightly

Music and lyrics by Debbie Friedman

CHORUS

On Tu B'Sh'-vat, on Tu B'Sh'-vat,

Watch the trees danc-ing in the breeze, Giv-ing shade to

you and__ me. The beau-ty that we come to see, That

comes from plant-ing just a seed._____

VERSE

1. And the earth will be hap-py,__ And the

earth will sing songs. We will plant our trees and

(CHORUS)

watch them blos-som, Giv-ing fruit, giv-ing gifts, grow-ing strong! On

2. And the trees will be happy,
   And the trees will sing songs,
   They will grow to be full of fruit so sweet,
   Caring for the hungry you and me!

Purim

Purim

Masks, Melodrama, and Merriment

The story Purim celebrates is as simple as a fairy tale. Once upon a time there was a wicked man named Haman. His job was to advise the absent-minded King Ahashverosh of Persia. When the king met Esther, a beautiful Jewish woman, he fell madly in love with her and made her his queen. Everything was fine until Esther's uncle Mordechai refused to bow before Haman. Jews bow only to God, not to people. Haman became so furious that he told the king to have all the Jews killed, and Ahashverosh agreed — not knowing that Esther was Jewish. Before Haman could carry out the king's orders, Esther told her husband the truth about herself. The king ordered the Jews to be spared and Haman to be hanged.

Purim, which comes in early spring, is a holiday of laughter, costumes, puppet shows, plays, and giving delicious treats to friends. Even though it is not a major holiday like Passover, Purim is a favorite, perhaps because it is so different from the other holidays. In fact, it's quite wild. When else is it all right to scream in the synagogue at the mention of a name? That's what happens when the Megillat Esther, or Book of Esther, is read on the eve of Purim. Whenever Haman's name is said, everyone yells and stamps their feet, sometimes with *Haman* written on the bottom of their shoe. Special Purim noise-makers called groggers are also rattled to drown out Haman's name. Adults traditionally are supposed to drink enough so that they cannot tell the difference between Mordechai and Haman.

Does it matter whether Mordechai, Haman, Ahashverosh, and Esther ever lived, that no one knows for sure? Why would a people who care so much about their history devote a holiday to what might be just a legend?

The writer Isaac Bashevis Singer once said: "A fact that is boring is not true." Purim may not be factual, but it is true. It tells the truth about what it has been like for Jews to live in many countries throughout the world. Sometimes Jews have been welcome, but too often they have been blamed for the country's problems. Whenever a persuasive leader like Haman has turned the king or the people against the Jews, their very lives have been endangered.

Until Haman became a powerful adviser to the king, the Jews of Persia felt like full citizens. But overnight, they were no longer Persians; they were only Jews. For Jews living outside Israel, the Purim story has special meaning. They understand the fear and helplessness of Mordechai and Esther when faced with a powerful villain.

Can you imagine how you might feel if you were picked on all the time and couldn't do anything about it? It could make you angry enough to hate those who hate you. Or you might hate yourself because if you were different, you wouldn't have this problem.

The Jewish people needed a way to live with people hating them and not be driven crazy by it. Every day they prayed for a better time, a time when they didn't have to beg to be treated decently. But one day a year they let go of being serious about this problem. Even in the worst times, it's good to remember how much fun life can be.

The Book of Esther

The Book of Esther isn't part of the Five Books of Moses that Jews call the Torah. Purim is less religious than the other holidays mentioned in the Torah — it's celebrated in disguise, often not in the synagogue or home but in the street. In fact, the Book of Esther doesn't even include God's name, and unlike the other books in the Bible, it is often richly illustrated.

Instead of God talking to the people and offering an outstretched arm, Esther speaks to the king and saves her people. Purim is not only about people playing an active part in their survival, it's about a woman hero. Esther, whose name means "star" in Persian, also had a Hebrew name, Hadassah, which means myrtle. She was beautiful, brave, and smart enough to know how to live in two worlds.

Purim means Casting of Lots, as in a lottery. Haman was going to draw lots to choose the day the Jews would be killed. Purim faces the difficult truth that life is uncertain, that sometimes things happen that don't make sense. One response to this randomness is to join in the upside-down nature of things and play with it. Another is to remember that, despite all the "random" events in the Purim story, the Jewish people survived.

On the evening of Purim, we get a vacation from being ourselves. We put on a costume of a villain or a hero, and go to the synagogue, where the rabbi may have switched places with the cantor, so the rabbi sings and the cantor, comically imitating the rabbi, leads the reading of the Scroll of Esther. Some people dress as Esther, Mordechai, or Haman, but you can disguise yourself as a pirate, robot, or anything you can imagine.

The afternoon of Purim, or the Sunday closest to it, is often a day of carnivals, parades, and costume parties. If Purim is a day of taking pleasure, it's also a day of *giving* pleasure: we perform *tzedakah* by donating food or money to at least two poor people, and we practice *mishloah manot* (gift giving) by bringing a plate of sweet treats to at least one friend.

Queen Esther's Story

A Play

CHARACTERS

KING AHASHVEROSH, ruler of Persia

QUEEN VASHTI, Ahashverosh's first wife

HAMAN, the king's adviser

MORDECHAI, a respected Jew

ESTHER, Mordechai's beautiful cousin

PARTY GUESTS

BEAUTY CONTESTANTS (Barbie dolls would be perfect.)

SETTING: Shushan, the capital of Persia twenty-five hundred years ago.

SCENE ONE. An exuberant party in the king's palace. The king and his friends are feasting, drinking, and talking noisily.

HAMAN: This is a great party, Your Royal Highness. Only one thing is missing: Queen Vashti.

AHASHVEROSH: Good idea, Haman. [*In a loud voice:*] Vashti! Come here and entertain us!

[*A long pause, then off-stage:*]

VASHTI: I'm your wife and queen, not your court clown. Go find someone else!

HAMAN: That's outrageous! What will you do to her, Your Lordship?

AHASHVEROSH: I don't need a queen like that — get rid of her, Haman.

A GUEST: But how will you find a new queen, Your Mightiness?

AHASHVEROSH: Hmm. [*Pause while he thinks.*] I know — I will hold a contest. Every woman in Persia will participate. I will choose the most beautiful woman in the land!

SCENE TWO. *Mordechai's house.*

ESTHER: No! Don't ask me again, Cousin Mordechai! I hate beauty contests, and even if it is the king's command, I won't go.
MORDECHAI: But you have to, dear Esther. You have no choice. Anyway, out of all the women in Persia, he probably won't choose you.
ESTHER: OK, OK. I'll go. But I won't even wear lipstick, and I'm not going to change my clothes!

SCENE THREE. *The palace. A line of women in jewelry and glittering gowns, except for Esther in a simple white dress. The king sits on a throne in front of them.*

AHASHVEROSH: [*Pointing*] The woman in white. She's the one I want.
[*The Jews of Persia cheer. This is the audience's part.*]
ESTHER: [*Softly*] Oh, no.

SCENE FOUR. *The palace six months later. The king and queen are holding hands because they have come to love each other.*

HAMAN: Excuse me, Your Kingship, but I have something of grave importance to tell you.
AHASHVEROSH: Speak, and it had better be *very* important.
HAMAN: There is a group of people in Shushan who have their own laws, a different god. They are dangerous, sire. Let me get rid of them.
AHASHVEROSH: Do your job, Haman, and don't bother me with these problems.

SCENE FIVE. *Outside the palace. A noose hangs from a tree.*

HAMAN: This is for that Jew, Mordechai, who refuses to bow to me. He will be the first Jew to hang, and I won't rest until they all are dead! The king told me to do my job, and that means getting rid of the Jews.

SCENE SIX. The palace.

MORDECHAI: Esther! Haman is plotting to kill all the Jews. You've got to tell the king!

ESTHER: Oh, no! The king doesn't even know that I'm Jewish. I'll do what I can.

SCENE SEVEN. The palace the next night. Queen Esther is having a banquet for the king. All the king's friends, and of course, Haman, are there.

AHASHVEROSH: My queen, you have given me a wonderful banquet. What can I give you in return?

ESTHER: O my worthy husband and king, grant me my life!

AHASHVEROSH: My dear, who threatens you?

ESTHER: Haman! He has decreed that on the fourteenth of Adar, all the Jews in Persia are to be killed. And, forgive me for not telling you until now, but I am Jewish!

AHASHVEROSH: Haman, you are a trickster and an evil man! That noose hanging outside the palace will be for you! Mordechai will replace you as my right-hand man.

ALL THE GUESTS: Yea, Mordechai! Yea, Ahashverosh! Bravo, Esther, our brave and beautiful queen!

How K'tonton Masqueraded on Purim

by Sadie Rose Weilerstein

K'TONTON WAS A TINY BOY, no bigger than your thumb.

"Father," said K'tonton, "when you were a little boy, did you dress up on Purim and wear a mask?"

"What a question!"

"And did you go to other people's houses and sing songs?"

"Of course!"

"Could I dress up and masquerade?"

"A little fellow like you, K'tonton? You would be left behind under a doormat. But I'll make you a grogger. That will be better than masquerading."

K'tonton's father took out a pen knife and a bit of wood and made him a beautiful noise-making grogger.

"*Ras! Ras! Ras!*" went the grogger as K'tonton whirled it about.

"It's nice to have a grogger," said K'tonton, "but not so nice as masquerading on Purim. I'd better talk to Mother."

Mother was in the kitchen rolling out *imberlah*. She lifted K'tonton to the table.

"Could I masquerade on Purim?" asked K'tonton.

"You?" said Mother. "Listen to the child! Haven't I lost you enough times already? But I'll tell you what I'll do. I'll make you a little *hamantasch* all for yourself. See! I've been pounding the poppy seeds." She pointed to a brass mortar on the table.

"Oh," said K'tonton, "poppy seed with honey?"

"Honey, of course," said Mother. "What else? Now sit still, K'tonton. I'll be back in a minute."

Off Mother went. K'tonton crossed his legs and waited.

"A minute is a long time," he said after a while.

He sat still again.

"I guess it must be two minutes. I guess it must be nine minutes. I guess I'll just get up and take a look at that poppy seed."

Up the side of a sack of flour he ran. Now he could see deep down into the mortar. He could see the pounder leaning against the side.

"That's a good slide," said K'tonton. He loved sliding down things. "I'll slide down and take a taste of that poppy seed. Mother wouldn't mind just a little taste."

The next minute his legs were over the top of the pestle and he was sliding down. A thought popped into his head. "I must stop before I reach the bottom. I might get stuck." But he couldn't stop. He was going too fast. *Blimp!* He was in poppy seed up to his waist.

And there was Mother's voice coming toward him. "Where's that K'tonton? I can't seem to keep track of him today. Well, I'll have to make the *hamantaschen* without him."

K'tonton felt the mortar lifted and turned over. The next moment he was tumbling head over heels into a big bowl with poppy seed all around him. You couldn't tell which was poppy seed and which was K'tonton.

"Mother! Mother!" K'tonton began, but a stream of honey was flowing over him. The words caught in the honey and stuck fast.

And now a big wooden spoon came down into the bowl. It picked K'tonton up. It tossed him! It chased him! Round and round went K'tonton with the wooden spoon close behind. It caught him at last. It lifted him up into the air. It set him down in the middle of something soft. Dough! A flat piece of dough! K'tonton was being made into a *hamantasch!*

"I must speak! I must call!" thought K'tonton. "My voice! Where is my voice?" It was gone. By the time it returned, he had been slipped into a pan and was being carried off.

A *hamantasch!* That meant he would be put into an oven, a fiery furnace like

Abraham and Daniel's companions. And God would not save him as He had saved Daniel's companions and Abraham. Had he not disobeyed his dear Mother?

"Dear God," K'tonton prayed, "save me from the fiery oven even if I don't deserve it."

A voice was speaking. K'tonton pressed his ear to the hole in the *hamantasch* and listened.

"I'll leave the cakes on the shelf here to rise." The pan was lifted. Then all was still.

Then he wasn't to be put into the oven, not for a little while at least. He might yet escape. But how! He tried to move. His arms were stuck fast to his sides.

"I'll eat my way out," said K'tonton. He ate and he ate and he ate. He ate so much he felt he could never look at honey or a poppy seed again. The hole grew bigger and bigger. It grew so big he could stick his head out, and he could wriggle his hands loose, his arms, his legs. He was free.

Far, far below was the table. K'tonton shut his eyes tight and jumped — safe into the middle of the sack of flour.

But his troubles were not yet over.

Creak, creak, came a step across the floor.

"Mother!" thought K'tonton. "I must hide until I get this poppy seed washed off."

He slipped onto a plate and hid behind a pile of *imberlah*.

Mother's voice came nearer. "Father," it said, "I'm going to take this *shloah manot* to the new little boy next door. He has been sick in bed ever since they moved in. Poor little fellow! The sweets may cheer him up a bit."

She threw a napkin over the plate.

"Look after K'tonton, Father," she said. "He's somewhere about."

She lifted the plate and was off. And there was K'tonton in the *shloah manot* dish with cakes and candies and *hamantaschen* all about him.

"I wonder what is going to happen next?" he thought.

He was so tired he snuggled down at the bottom of the dish and shut his eyes. In another minute he was asleep.

"What has happened? Where am I?" said K'tonton when he opened his eyes a little later.

He peered cautiously over the side of a *hamantasch* and looked about. He was in a strange room. The dish was lying on a table near a bed, and on the bed lay a young boy propped up with pillows. Such a pale, unhappy-looking little fellow! He was staring soberly at the *shloah manot*, at the cakes, the Purim candies, the *hamantaschen*, but he did not taste a thing and there wasn't a smile on his face. Something hurt inside of K'tonton.

"One oughtn't to look like that on Purim," he thought. "Purim is a good day, a day of gladness and feasting, a day of sending gifts to one another. The Megillah says it is."

K'tonton forgot that he was supposed to be hiding. He forgot he was covered with poppy seed. He forgot that he was dusted with flour. He knew only that he had to make that little boy smile. He stepped from behind the *hamantasch* and bowed low.

The boy's mouth opened and his eyes grew as big as saucers.

"The inside of a *hamantasch* came alive!"

He stared hard.

"It must be a toy," he decided. "I suppose there are springs inside." He reached out his hand to feel, but K'tonton sprang back.

"I'm not a toy," he said. "I'm not the inside of a *hamantasch*, though I was inside one," he added truthfully. "I-I" — it was then that the great thought dawned on him — "I'm a Purim masquerader and I'm dressed up in poppy seed and I've come to other people's houses, to your house, to sing Purim songs."

At that he lifted his shrill voice and began to sing:

Happy, happy Purim

Happy Purim day!

For a minute the boy sat perfectly still and stared. Then he threw his head back and laughed. Such a happy, jolly, hearty, rollicking laugh, a regular Purim laugh! "Ha, Ha, Ha, Ha, Ha, Ha! Ho, Ho, Ho, He, He!"

"What could have happened?" cried the little boy's mother, who was in the next room. "I haven't heard David laugh in weeks."

She hurried into the bedroom, and K'tonton's mother followed her. There was David, laughing and clapping his hands; and there in the middle of the *shloah manot* dish, black with poppy seed, dusted with flour, was a wee little fellow, singing and dancing away.

"K'tonton!" cried his mother. "How did you get here? What does this mean?"

"I-I'm the inside of a *hamantasch*," said K'tonton. "I'm in other people's houses. I'm masquerading as you did when you were a little girl."

"Please let him stay, please," begged David. "We're having such a jolly time."

So K'tonton's mother hurried home and fetched him a clean little suit and blouse and scrubbed him and dressed him in his holiday clothes.

K'tonton's father came too. He brought a Megillah with him and sang them the whole story of Purim, all about the King and Mordechai and the wicked Haman, and how good Queen Esther saved the Jews. K'tonton ran along under the words in the Megillah — to keep the place, you know — and every time he came to the name of the wicked Haman he whirled his grogger — *Ras! Ras! Ras!*

Then they sang songs and ate the cakes and *imberlah* and *hamantaschen*; and everybody had such a happy time that no one thought of scolding K'tonton at all.

*Here are two ideas that will get you right
into the wild and crazy Purim spirit!*

Purim Puppets

If you have dolls at home, even action figures, you can put on your own Purim puppet show using the script on page 79. All you need are a few scraps of fabric. Make two crowns out of aluminum foil, one for Queen Esther and one for King Ahashverosh. Dress Esther in a long white gown made of fabric or a tissue, and put a purple or blue robe on the king. Uncle Mordechai needs a full beard of cotton, and Haman is dressed all in black. Don't forget Haman's triangle hat. Now you have the players — let the play begin!

Groggers

This noisemaker will give you years of noise, yet only takes a few minutes to make. You need an empty aluminum soda can and twelve pennies. Put the pennies in the can and shake it. It will make quiet dogs bark, barking dogs quiet, and will absolutely drown out "HAMAN!" If you want to decorate the can, spray-paint it gold, and with a purple permanent marker, draw crowns, *hamantaschen*, and Stars of David on it. I suggest purple because it is the color of royal robes.

You can also use tambourines, drums, horns, or cymbals to overpower Haman's name with music.

Hamantaschen

Hamantaschen *means Haman's pockets, but really, the triangle-shaped cookies look like the hat Haman supposedly wore. The cookies are as sweet as the day, filled with either a poppy seed or fruit mixture (usually prune).*

HONEY DOUGH

4 cups flour

1 teaspoon baking soda

½ teaspoon salt

4 eggs

1 cup honey

¼ pound butter, melted

Preheat the oven to 350°F.

Sift the dry ingredients together into a large bowl. Add the eggs, honey, and butter, and mix. Roll out on a lightly floured board. This is a very sticky dough; you might need to add a little flour to get the dough flat. With a glass of a diameter of three or four inches, cut circles in the dough, rolling it out again and again until it is all in circles. Put a little filling in the center of each circle, and fold the edges to make three corners. Bake for 30 minutes. Let the *hamantaschen* cool, and give them away to your friends and family. Makes about 48 cookies.

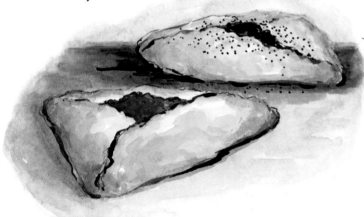

POPPY SEED FILLING

2 cups poppy seeds

1 cup water

½ cup honey

¼ cup sugar

¼ teaspoon salt

In a small saucepan or a teapot, bring the water to a boil. Put the seeds in a strainer, and pour the boiling water over them. Drain well. Grind the seeds in a mortar or food processor. Place the ground seeds in a medium-size saucepan, add the other ingredients, and cook over a low flame, stirring, until thick.

PRUNE FILLING

1 pound cooked prunes

1 teaspoon grated orange rind

½ cup nuts

¼ teaspoon salt

¼ teaspoon vanilla extract

In a large bowl, chop the prunes, then add the other ingredients, and mix well.

(About these fillings: any fruit preserves, such as apricot or raspberry jam or orange marmalade, can be used, too. And poppy seed filling comes already made, in a can. You might find it in a store with international foods or at a kosher butcher.)

Pesah

Pesah

A Season of Freedom

Pesah, or Passover, the oldest Jewish holiday, celebrates the beginning of the Jewish people. It was on Passover three thousand years ago at midnight, under the first full moon of spring, that the Israelites escaped from Egyptian slavery. During the week-long holiday, which falls on the fifteenth of Nisan (late March to mid-April), Jews remember the power and importance of this event by eating special foods linked to the bitterness of slavery and the sweetness of freedom.

The highlight of Passover is the seder, a dramatic yet playful dinner rich with stories, food, and song. *Seder* means order, and a book called a Haggadah takes participants through the fifteen steps of the evening celebration that retells the story of how the Jews became a free people. The ceremony begins by reliving slavery and ends by imagining what the world will be like when all people are free.

The seder is often long, but it should also be fun, and above all, intriguing, even to the youngest at the table, because the ceremony is supposed to teach everyone about the Exodus from Egypt. More than just a lesson, the story needs to become part of each listener.

Children are central to the seder. The youngest child asks four questions, beginning with "Why is this night different from all others?" A child opens the door to welcome the prophet Elijah, and a child ends the seder by finding the hidden piece of matzah called the *afikomen*.

Children are essential to the holiday because Passover celebrates birth. Although Moses isn't mentioned in the Haggadah — to remind the Jewish people that God, not Moses, led them out of Egypt — the story of his birth is a key part of the story of Passover. When a baby is born, the sac that protects

the embryo breaks, and fluid flows from the mother. When the waters of the Red Sea broke apart, the Jewish people were born.

Besides celebrating the birth of the Jewish people, Passover celebrates spring. Just as God freed the Jews from Egypt, so spring frees the earth from winter each year. From the first green shoots of barley that break the earth's cold surface, to the first calves that break out of the womb, spring is a time of freedom and birth.

Passover also marks the beginning of the harvest season. Twenty-five hundred years ago, on the second day of Passover, everyone brought an *omer*, a sheaf of barley, to the ancient Temple in Jerusalem. This offering began "the counting of the *omer*," a forty-nine-day period between Passover and Shavuot. To keep count of the days, people use decorative *omer* calendars, some of which can be colored in daily, making a bright pattern by the time Shavuot rolls around.

Breaking Out

Let my people go!
Exodus 5:1

When the children of Israel first came to Egypt thirty-three hundred years ago, they were not a nation or a people. They were just a large hungry family looking for a place to feed their flocks of sheep. Their relative Joseph, a valued adviser in the court of the pharaoh, Egypt's king, had invited them to settle in nearby Goshen. Within a generation the Israelites became a prosperous, hard-working part of Egyptian society. They were different from the Egyptians because they spoke Hebrew and worshiped one God instead of the many Egyptian gods, but Pharaoh let them live as they chose.

By the time Joseph and the pharaoh died, hundreds of Israelites lived in Egypt. A new pharaoh came to power who had not known Joseph and who mistrusted his family. Fearing that its wealth and large population would give the Israelites — or Hebrews, as they were also called — the strength to rise up and join Egyptian enemies, he tried to weaken them by reducing their numbers.

First, he ordered the Hebrews to leave Goshen to help the Egyptians fortify the cities of Pithom and Raamses against any attacks. He ordered the Israelites to mold bricks of clay and straw and to build pyramids with the bricks. The Israelites gradually became Pharaoh's slaves. He was sure that sixteen-hour work days in hot fields would weaken their bodies and break their spirits. They would not have the strength to create children and their population would dwindle.

The Israelites, however, still bore children despite their hard labor. Pharaoh took harsher measures and separated husbands from wives during the week.

This also did not work, because the Hebrew women foiled Pharaoh by visiting their husbands each day, supposedly to bring them lunch. In this way they continued to become pregnant and bear children.

Pharaoh suspected that there was something strange about the way these people kept multiplying, and he feared them. When one of his astrologers told him that some day a male Israelite would rise up and free his people, Pharaoh wanted every Hebrew male infant to be killed. The midwives, women who helped at childbirth, were secretly ordered to take the newborn sons from their mothers immediately after birth and throw them into the Nile River. They were to tell each mother that her baby had been stillborn.

Despite Pharaoh's command, however, Israelite boy infants continued to survive. Pharaoh sent for the midwives and demanded an explanation. Appealing to his hatred of the Israelites, the midwives lied and told him that the Hebrew women, unlike the delicate, refined Egyptian women, were like animals. They had their babies quickly and hid them before the midwives arrived. The truth was that the midwives had been secretly saving these babies because they could not bring themselves to kill them.

Now Pharaoh dropped his shrewd and sly ways and told all Egyptians to drown every newborn Israelite boy in the Nile. Egyptians went into houses where they suspected a baby boy was being hidden. They brought along their own babies and pinched them to make them cry. When the hidden Hebrew baby heard the Egyptian babies' cries, he would cry, too. Then the Egyptians would take away the Hebrew boy.

Amram, a Hebrew, was worried that his wife, Jocheved, might give birth to a son, so he told her that they should have no more children. They would have to be satisfied with their only child, Miriam. But Jocheved protested, saying that Amram was worse than Pharaoh because he wanted to eliminate *all* Hebrew babies, not just sons. She convinced Amram to have another child, who turned out to be a boy. Jocheved hid her baby as best she could, but at three months he was too lively to be kept hidden. So she wove a basket of bulrushes, sealed the inside with tree sap to make it float, covered the inside with soft blankets, and put the baby into it. She hoped that the basket would float long enough on the Nile for someone to take pity on the baby and rescue him.

Miriam took the basket to the Nile and placed it near the river's edge. Then she hid in the bushes to see if anyone would rescue her brother. Before long Pharaoh's childless daughter came to bathe and heard the baby crying. Guessing immediately that it was a Hebrew child, she lifted it from the water. At that moment Miriam appeared and asked the princess, "Shall I get a Hebrew nurse to care for this child for you?"

The princess agreed and Miriam ran home to get Jocheved.

"Take this child and nurse it for me, and I will pay your wages because I've always wanted a child," Pharaoh's daughter told a relieved and joyful Jocheved.

When the baby was three and no longer needed to be nursed, Jocheved brought him to Pharaoh's daughter. She called him her son and named him Moses, which the rabbis translated as "I drew him out of the water."

Although Moses was loved and treated well in Pharaoh's palace, he remembered his mother and never forgot that he was an Israelite. It hurt him to see his people so harshly treated. One day he walked out to the fields where the Israelites were building a pyramid. There Moses saw an Egyptian taskmaster whip an old man for working too slowly. Moses was so enraged that he struck and killed the taskmaster.

Moses's moment of anger ended his life of privilege. If the Egyptian soldiers caught him, he would be executed. So Moses fled to nearby Midian. There he married Zipporah, a Midianite shepherdess, had a son, Gershom, and lived the quiet, peaceful life of a shepherd. He worked for his father-in-law, Jethro, a Midianite priest, and was far from the troubles of the Israelites in Egypt.

One day while taking care of his sheep, Moses sat down and looked at the lovely hills surrounding Midian. Suddenly he caught sight of a thornbush burning more brightly than any fire that he had ever seen. He turned his eyes away at first, and then looked again. The bush was burning, yet it was not burning up. Moses heard a voice call, "Moses! Moses!"

Moses answered, "Here I am." The voice told him to remove his sandals because the ground upon which he was standing was holy.

When the voice said, "I am the God of your father, the God of Abraham, the God of Isaac, and the God of Jacob," Moses hid his face. He was terrified. But

he stayed and listened to God tell him to be His holy messenger. God had heard the groans of the Hebrews and wanted to rescue them by leading them from Egypt into a new land that flowed with milk and honey. "Come, therefore," God said, "I will send you to Pharaoh, and you shall free My people, the Israelites, from Egypt."

But Moses hesitated. "Please, O Lord," he replied, "I have never been a man of words; I am slow of speech and slow of tongue." He feared that neither the Hebrews nor Pharaoh would listen to him. Pharaoh didn't even believe that the Hebrew God existed.

God dismissed his protests. "Who gives man speech? Who makes him dumb or deaf, seeing or blind? Is it not I, the Lord?" God assured Moses that He would tell him what to say, and that Aaron, Moses's brother, could speak for him. It would be God's power, not Moses's power, that would persuade Pharaoh and convince the Hebrews. After all, God chose the lowly thornbush to represent Him when He spoke to Moses.

Moses returned to Egypt with his wife and son. When he went to see Pharaoh to tell him that the God of Israel wanted His people to leave Egypt, Pharaoh refused. Not only did he refuse, but he made the lives of the Israelites worse. He ordered them to make bricks, but he no longer gave them straw. They had to find straw and somehow make the same number of bricks as before. The exhausted Israelites blamed Moses for the extra work.

They told him that they didn't want his help. Even though their lives were terrible, they were managing to survive. They didn't know if Moses could give them a better life.

Moses would gladly have given up his job of being God's messenger, but God would not let him. To reassure Moses and his reluctant followers, God described in four different ways how He would help them:

1. I will free you from the burdens of the Egyptians.

2. I will deliver you from their bondage.

3. I will redeem you with an outstretched arm and through extraordinary chastisements.

4. I will take you to be My people, and I will be your God.

"Pharaoh is stubborn," God told Moses. "He refuses to let the people go." Moses would have to convince Pharaoh that there was only one God, whose might was greater than anyone's, including Pharaoh's. It would take "extraordinary chastisements," ten plagues, each more terrible than the next, before Pharaoh would relent.

The plagues were the consequence of Pharaoh's cruelty. Of all sins, the rabbis believed slavery was the most hideous because being master over another human being was the same as trying to be God.

Moses warned Pharaoh that God would turn the water of the Nile into blood, and that it would smell and be undrinkable. But Pharaoh didn't heed his warning. So, for seven days, the Nile was turned to blood, the fish were made to die, and the people had to dig frantically for water. Pharaoh thought it was no more than a simple magic trick that his own magicians could have performed. He refused to let the Israelites go.

In the second plague, God made frogs infest everything from food and beds to people's clothing. This time Pharaoh told Moses if his God could get rid of the frogs, Pharaoh would let the Hebrews leave. Moses gladly replied, "So that you know that there is none like the Lord, the frogs shall retreat from you and your people; they shall remain only in the Nile." But, once the frogs had disappeared, Pharaoh took back his promise and became stubborn again.

For the third plague, God sent lice to every animal and person so that they itched horribly. Pharaoh's magicians were frightened and said it was the finger of God, but Pharaoh was unmoved.

So God sent a fourth plague — swarms of buzzing flies over Egypt. But He didn't send them to Goshen, where the children of Israel lived. Again, Pharaoh promised to let the Israelites go if the flies left Egypt but, as soon as they were gone, he changed his mind and hardened his heart.

Then, in the fifth plague, God infected and killed all the livestock in Egypt, except for those of the Israelites. Still Pharaoh would not let the Israelites go.

God then sent a sixth plague, which caused every human being and animal in Egypt to be covered with painful skin boils. But Pharaoh's heart remained hard.

God sent a seventh plague — heavy hail with thunder and lightning that killed all living things that were left outdoors, everywhere but in the land of Goshen.

Now Pharaoh began to be afraid. He summoned Moses and begged him to tell his God to stop the hail. He would free the Israelites. Moses stopped the hail, but again Pharaoh changed his mind.

The Lord sent an eighth plague, and locusts covered the land so thickly that they made a black moving carpet over Egypt. They ate all the trees and filled the palaces and houses. When they were done eating, nothing green remained. Again Pharaoh begged Moses to get rid of the plague, and again he changed his mind when the plague was past. Pharaoh refused to learn his lesson.

Then, in the ninth plague, God laid a dark fog across Egypt that was so thick that none of the Egyptians could see each other. God protected the Israelites, however, giving them light. As soon as Pharaoh told Moses he could have his wish, Pharaoh went back on his word another time.

The tenth plague was the most dreadful of all. God warned that He would take the firstborn animal and person from every house if Pharaoh would not free the Israelites. Slaves and kings would suffer equally.

God told Moses to tell each Hebrew family to prepare to flee that night. They were to pack up their belongings, slaughter a lamb, and take its blood to mark the doorposts of their houses. The Angel of Death would "pass over" the marked houses.

The Israelites knew by the crying all around them that the Angel of Death was near. When Pharaoh lost his only child, he called Moses to the palace and told him to take his people out of Egypt immediately. After two hundred years of slavery, the Hebrews — six hundred thousand of them, according to the Torah — left Egypt guided by a bright full moon. They took their cattle and whatever they could carry, including dough that hadn't had time to rise. Their suffering had united them as a people, with Moses as their leader.

Their misery wasn't over yet, however. Once again Pharaoh changed his mind and sent his soldiers to stop the Israelites. As the Hebrews got to the Red Sea, they heard the thunder of Pharaoh's army behind them. They were afraid that they would drown in the sea or be slaughtered by the soldiers. Miraculously, a strong wind came up to part the Red Sea, and the Israelites walked on the floor of the sea with walls of water on either side. After they crossed safely, the water closed and the Egyptians drowned.

The death of the Egyptians diminished the Israelites' joy in victory. When the Egyptians were drowning in the Red Sea, the angels in heaven were about to sing triumphantly, but God silenced them, saying, "My creatures are perishing, and you are ready to sing!" In this spirit, at the seder a drop of wine is spilled for each plague. Because the Egyptians suffered, the Jews cannot rejoice completely.

The slavery of the Israelites is not a happy or proud memory in Jewish history, but it has given the Jewish people sympathy for others in bondage. More than a historical recollection, Passover is also a reminder that there are still slaves in the world who need help.

The great teacher Hillel said, "If I am not for myself, who will be for me? And if I am only for myself, what am I?" On Passover, Jews pray that the festive meal and its memories will give them the strength to fight for freedom in the world.

The Seder Table

The seder table is beautiful but unusual. At first glance it looks as though it's set for a dinner party, but, in addition to fancy dishes and flowers on the table, there are many special things about it. Even though it is an evening celebration, there is a place set for the youngest child. A pillow rests on the chair of the leader of the seder. This is not to prop up a tired leader but to symbolize freedom. A free person can be comfortable and recline, while a slave can never relax.

The Seder Plate

On Passover Jews eat history. Israel Zangwill

In front of the leader's place is a large ornate plate that displays five important symbols of Passover. First there are small white bits of root, which look deceptively mild. These are *maror*, or bitter herbs, eaten to remember the bitterness of Egyptian bondage. The power of the herb, which is often horseradish, is astounding. Romaine lettuce is also used as *maror*, because at first it tastes sweet, and then it turns bitter. In the beginning, the Israelites' life in Egypt was sweet, and then it turned bitter.

The next object on the plate is a brownish, unappetizing-looking mixture called *haroset*. This mixture is also deceptive because it is delicious. It is supposed to look like the mortar that the Israelites used to build the cities of Pithom and Raamses. Made of apples, nuts, cinnamon, and wine, its sweetness represents the promise of a better world. The mixture is also a reminder of the apple trees under which Israelite women bore their children, away from the eyes of the Egyptians.

The shank bone of a lamb, called the *z'roah*, lies beside the *haroset*. This symbolizes the lamb eaten in haste when the Israelites fled Egypt. The shank bone is used because "the Lord, our God, brought us forth with a strong hand and an outstretched arm." The bone is a reminder of God's arm.

Next to the shank bone is a roasted egg, called the *beitzah*. It is a symbol of the animal sacrifice that was brought to the Temple for each festival. The egg is also a symbol of life. One midrash, or legend, draws a connection between the egg and the Jews. Just as an egg gets harder as it cooks, so the Jewish people grew harder the more tyrants throughout history tried to weaken them.

Last there is *karpas*, fresh greens that are usually parsley, celery, or lettuce. *Karpas*, which is a Greek word meaning hors d'oeuvre, is a symbol of new life in nature and the new life for the Jewish people when they were freed from bondage. The *karpas* is dipped in salt water, which represents the tears of slavery.

Matzah

Jews eat matzah, flat, bumpy bread, during the week of Passover to remember that their ancestors didn't have time to let their bread dough rise before they fled Egypt. Matzah was the plain, humble food of slaves, but it also recalls the great moment of freedom.

Leavened bread is puffed up and fancier than matzah; it symbolizes self-importance. Matzah teaches about the simplicity and humility of the poor. It is a natural food that recalls a time when additives such as leavening weren't necessary. Passover is a time to examine oneself for signs of being inflated with too much pride and weighed down by too many things.

Next to the seder plate are three matzot, two for the blessing and one which will be broken by the leader as part of the ceremony. Two whole matzot are blessed because, when the Jews were in the wilderness, God gave them a double portion of manna, their survival food, on the Sabbath and festivals. The three matzot also represent the three remaining tribes of Israel: Kohen, Levi, and Yisrael. Because all Jews belong to one of these groups, it is as if the entire community of Israel sits at the seder table.

Haggadah

At the beginning of the seder, instead of food on each plate, there is a book. This is a sign that this will be more than just a dinner party. It will be a "talk-feast," almost a play, where people question, learn, and exchange ideas. The book is called a Haggadah, which means "the telling." It tells the story of the Exodus and is a guide to the seder. The first Haggadah was written one thousand years ago, when the rabbis feared that the story and the seder would be forgotten. Since then, three thousand editions have been written, each filled with history, literature, legend, folktales, and songs. Artists and writers have been inspired by the holiday to create beautiful Haggadot, each with slightly different interpretations. All add to the richness of the holiday.

Leading a Seder

Who leads a seder? Anyone in the family, or maybe several members. Each family, contributing its own customs and style, has given the holiday its richness and depth. There is no one way to conduct the seder and no rabbi to lead the service. The family members choose which Haggadah to use, or they may create their own. This is important, because a free person makes choices. *Seder* means order. It is the sequence of the evening's events, but it also sparks new ideas and individual expression.

The Four Questions

The story of the Exodus is started by a child, not by the leader. The youngest person at the table asks the leader four important questions about why this night is different from all the others in the year. For the child, the greatest difference is that, for one wonderful moment, everyone listens to him or her. The questions are asked in Hebrew, and then they're repeated in English:

1. Why is this night different from all other nights? On all other nights, we eat either leavened or unleavened bread; why, on this night, do we eat only matzah, which is unleavened bread?

2. On all other nights, we eat vegetables and herbs of all kinds; why, on this night, do we eat bitter herbs especially?

3. On all other nights, we never think of dipping herbs in the water or anything else; why, on this night, do we dip the parsley in salt water and the bitter herbs in *haroset?*

4. On all other nights, everyone sits up straight at the table; why, on this night, do we recline at the table?

Elijah's Cup

One cup of wine stands alone in the center of the table. This cup is for Elijah, the prophet who, according to Jewish teaching, will announce the coming of the Messiah. Elijah also helps the poor, and in legends he appears at the last moment to save starving families. The rabbis said that the Messiah will come when there are no hungry people in the world. Each year at Passover, everyone watches Elijah's cup carefully to see if he has come to drink the wine and bring us closer to a more generous world. This is the message of Passover: we will all be free when we are willing to share with one another.

Some families take Elijah's cup, which has been empty, and pass it around the table. Then, while they open the door and sing, "Eliahu Ha-Navi" (Elijah the Prophet) to welcome him, participants pour a little wine from their cups into Elijah's cup—showing that the Messiah will come when each of us becomes a partner in bringing holiness to the world.

Opening the door for Elijah began for a frightening reason. In the Middle Ages, a rumor spread that the Jews used the blood of Christian children for the Passover celebration. This blood libel, as it was called, was absolutely false. Jewish law considers blood impure; in fact, blood from animals must be drained from meat before it's eaten. Still, ignorant people believed the rumor, so Jews opened the door at the seder to show that they had nothing to hide. They even drank white wine instead of red wine so that there would be no suspicion that they were drinking blood. Opening the door for Elijah may have begun because of a lie, but it became a gesture that expressed hope for a better world.

Afikomen

The *afikomen* (the word means "dessert") is a half piece of matzah that the leader sets aside at the beginning of the seder to be eaten at the end of the meal. The leader of the seder hides the *afikomen,* and the children hunt for it. When they find it, the leader asks for for it back, and the children bargain for a treat before they return it.

No one knows how this part of the seder began. Some believe its purpose, like much of the seder, is to keep the children awake and curious throughout the evening. Others find deeper meaning to the hide-and-seek game. The hidden *afikomen* is like the mysterious order of the universe, waiting to be uncovered. Children search for the *afikomen* because everyone is a child in search of the unknown.

The *afikomen* was a good-luck charm for Middle Eastern Jews. They thought a piece of it carried in a pocket would ward off illness and shipwrecks. Kurdish Jews bound a piece to a grown son's arm and said, "May you be as close to your wife."

Shmurah Matzah

During Passover, Jews are not to eat or own any hametz, *which means leaven.* Hametz *can be one or more of the following five grains mixed with water for eighteen minutes or more: wheat, rye, barley, oats, or spelt. Jews must also get rid of any food made with these grains, such as cookies, bread, pretzels, and bagels. Scrubbing the kitchen and putting out special dishes are part of making the house ready for Passover. Any food brought into the clean kitchen must be kosher for Passover, which includes matzah. Matzah contains wheat, but it is made in less than eighteen minutes. The following story is a comic reminder not to forget the deepest reason for eating matzah: to remember the bitterness of slavery and to work toward setting people free.*

Rabbi Israel was the most famous matzah supervisor in the world, renowned for his care in making sure the matzah was baked according to the strictest interpretation of law. Just enough water, just enough flour, just enough time in the oven to make it *shmurah* matzah, guarded matzah.

When the rabbi became ill just before Passover, everyone worried, "Who will supervise the matzah?"

"Shlomo and Yussel will do a fine job," the old rabbi said. And he took his pupils to the matzah-baking factory to learn their task.

The young men felt honored but terrified. They followed the rabbi from step to step, listening to his every word. Still they asked a million questions: "Rabbi, how much water? How long should the dough be kneaded? How long in the oven?" And so on and so on until the rabbi held up his hands and they stopped.

"See that old woman in the corner?" The rabbi pointed. The pupils nodded. "She is a widow and she is poor. See that she gets paid sufficiently — that will make the matzah the purest in the world."

The Carp in the Bathtub

by Barbara Cohen

WHEN I WAS A LITTLE GIRL, I lived in an apartment house in New York City with Mama and Papa and my little brother Harry.

It was not very fancy, but Papa said we were lucky. We had our own bathroom. Mrs. Ginzburg, who lived downstairs, was also lucky — she had one too. Everyone else had to share the bathrooms in the hall.

Mama was a wonderful cook. It was well known that she made the finest chicken soup in Flatbush. Also very good *tsimmis*, noodle *kugel, mondel* bread, and stuffed cabbage.

But best of all was Mama's gefilte fish. Twice a year she made gefilte fish — in the fall for Rosh Hashanah, the Jewish New Year, and in the spring for Pesah, the festival of Passover. Aunt Malke and Uncle Moishe, cousin Zipporah, and Papa's friend Mr. Teitelbaum always came to our house for the seder on the first night of Passover. They said that Mama's gefilte fish was not merely the best in Flatbush, nor the best in Brooklyn, but actually the best gefilte fish in all of New York City.

Harry and I loved the seder because we got to stay up until midnight. It took that long to say all the prayers, read the Passover story out of a book called the Haggadah, sing all the songs, and eat all the food. But I will tell you a secret. I was nine years old at the time I am telling you about, and I had never put a single piece of my mother's gefilte fish into my mouth.

Mama made her gefilte fish out of carp. For a day or two before Passover, carp was hard to find in the stores. All the ladies in the neighborhood had been buying it for their own gefilte fish. Mama liked to buy *her* carp at least a week before Passover to make sure she got the nicest, fattest, shiniest one. But Mama knew that a dead fish sitting in the icebox for a week would not be very good when the time came to make it into gefilte fish.

So Mama bought her fish live, and carried it home in a pail of water. All the way home it flopped and flipped because it was too big for the bucket. It would have died if Mama had left it in there.

As soon as she got home she would call, "Leah, run the water in the tub."

And I would put the rubber stopper in the drain and run some cold water into the bathtub. Then Mama would dump the carp out of the pail and into the tub.

The carp loved it there. He was always a big fish, but the tub was about four times as long as he was, and there was plenty of room for him to swim around.

Harry and I loved the carp. As long as he was there, we didn't have to take baths.

Most of our friends took baths only once a week, but because we had our own tub, Mama made us bathe twice a week. "Otherwise," she said, "what is the use of having our own bathroom?" We didn't think it was fair, and we would gladly have moved into an apartment where tenants shared the bathrooms in the hall.

Except, of course, when we had a carp living in our bathtub. Every time Harry or I had to go to the toilet, we would grab a crust of bread or a rusty lettuce leaf from the kitchen. While we sat on the toilet, we fed the bread or the lettuce leaf to the carp. This made going to the bathroom really fun, instead of just a waste of time.

But the day always came when Mama marched into the bathroom carrying a big metal strainer and removed the stopper from the tub. The carp always seemed to know what was coming. He swam away from her as fast as he could, splashing the water all over her apron with his strong, flat tail. But he didn't have a chance. Before all the water was even out of the tub, Mama had caught him in her strainer. The way he was flopping around, he would have been on the floor before Mama got out the bathroom door, so she dumped him right into her bucket and carried him to the kitchen.

We knew what she did with him when she got there, although we would never look. She killed him with a club! Then she scraped off the scales with a huge knife. The head, skin, and bones she boiled along with some carrots and onions in a big kettle of water to make stock. She put the flesh through a meat grinder with some more onions. After she had mixed it with matzah meal, eggs, and spices, she made it into balls. She took the stock and put it through the strainer to remove all the skin and bones, which she threw in the garbage.

She saved the stock for cooking the fish balls, which took hours. Harry and I would run out into the hall, but even there we couldn't escape the smell of fish.

Mama once told us that her Mama had not thrown away the skin. She had removed it so carefully from the carp that after the fish was cooked, she could put it back in the skin and bring it to the table. That's why the fish is called *gefilte*, Mama said, which means "stuffed." At least Harry and I were spared that!

You can see why we managed never to eat gefilte fish on Rosh Hashanah or Passover. Could *you* eat a friend?

The year I was nine was the worst of all. Most people think that all fish are pretty much the same, but this is definitely not true. Some carp are much more lovable than others, and that Passover we had an unusually playful and intelligent carp in our bathtub. He was larger than the others too. We were having extra company that year. Mrs. Ginzburg from downstairs and her unmarried daughter Elvira were coming up. Mr. Ginzburg had died six months before, and Mrs. Ginzburg just didn't have the heart to fuss and prepare for Passover.

This particular carp was also shinier than the others. His eyes were brighter and he seemed much livelier and friendlier. It got so that whenever Harry or I went into the bathroom, he'd swim right over to the end of the tub nearest the toilet as if he knew we were going to feed him. There was something about his mouth that made him seem to be smiling at us after he had eaten his bread crust or his lettuce.

In those days people like us, who lived in apartments in Flatbush, did not have pets. Harry and I would have loved owning a dog, cat, or a bird, but

Mama and Papa had never thought of such a thing, and it never occurred to us to ask. I'll tell you one thing, though. After that carp had been in our bathtub for nearly a week, we knew he was not just any old carp. He was our pet. In memory of Mr. Ginzburg, we called him Joe.

Two days before Passover, when I came home from school, Mama said, "You look after Harry, Leah. I have to go shopping, and I'll never get anything done if I have him trailing after me."

As soon as Mama was gone, I looked at Harry, and Harry looked at me.

"We have to save Joe," I told him.

"We'll never have another chance," Harry agreed. "But what'll we do?"

"Mrs. Ginzburg has a bathtub," I reminded him.

Harry nodded. He saw what I meant right away.

I went to the kitchen, got the bucket, and carried it to the bathroom. Harry had already let all the water out of the tub. He helped lift Joe into the bucket. It was not easy for us because Joe must have weighed fifteen pounds, but we finally managed. We could add only a little water to the pail because it was already almost too heavy for us.

With both of us holding on to the handle and banging the bucket against every step, we lugged it downstairs to Mrs. Ginzburg's door. Then we rang her bell. She was very fat, and it took her a long time to waddle to the door, but she finally opened it.

"Why, Leah, Harry!" she said in surprise. "I'm very glad to see you. Won't you come in? Why are you carrying that bucket?" Mrs. Ginzburg was a very nice lady. She was always kind to us, even when she couldn't understand what we were doing.

We carried our bucket into Mrs. Ginzburg's front room. "May I ask what you have there?" she said politely.

"It's Joe," said Harry.

"Joe!" Mrs. Ginzburg closed her eyes and put her hand over her heart.

"We named him for Mr. Ginzburg," I explained quickly. "He smiles like Mr. Ginzburg."

"Oh . . ." Mrs. Ginzburg tried to smile too. Just then Joe twitched, his tail flashed over the top of the bucket, and a few drops of water dripped onto the

Oriental rug Mrs. Ginzburg had bought at Abraham and Straus with Mr. Ginzburg's Christmas bonus two years before. She glanced into the pail. "My goodness," she said, "he looks like a fish to me."

"He is a fish," I said. "He's the best fish in the world, and Mama can't kill him for Passover. She just can't. Please let him stay in your bathtub. Please. Just for a little while. Until I can figure out where to keep him for good."

"But Leah," Mrs. Ginzburg said, "I can't do that. Your Mama is my dear friend."

"If you don't let us put Joe in your bathtub soon," Harry pleaded, "he'll be dead. He's almost dead now."

Mrs. Ginzburg and I peered into the bucket. Harry was right. Joe didn't look too good. His scales weren't shiny bright anymore, and he had stopped thrashing around. There was not enough water in the bucket for him.

"All right," said Mrs. Ginzburg. "But just for now." She ran some water into her tub, and we dumped our carp in. He no sooner felt all that clear cold water around him than he perked right up and started swimming. I took a few

morsels of chopped meat I had stored away in my dress pocket and gave them to him. He smiled at me, just like always.

"This fish can't stay here," Mrs. Ginzburg warned. "I'm afraid I can't help hide him from your mother and father."

"What shall we do?" Harry asked me, blinking his eyes hard to keep back the tears.

"We'll go find Papa," I told him. "Papa doesn't cook, so maybe he'll understand. We'll have to find him before Mama gets home."

Papa was a cutter in a garment factory in Manhattan. He came home every night on the subway. Harry and I went down to the corner and waited by the stairs that led up from the station. After a while, we saw a big crowd of people who had just gotten off the train come up the stairs. Papa was with them. He was holding on to the rail and climbing slowly, with his head down.

"Papa, Papa," we called.

He looked up and saw us. He straightened his shoulders, smiled, and ran quickly up the few remaining steps. "You came to meet me," he said. "That's very nice."

We started home together. I was holding one of Papa's hands, and Harry was holding the other. "Papa," I asked, "do you like gefilte fish?"

"Why, yes," he said, "of course I like gefilte fish. Your mother makes the best gefilte fish in all of Flatbush — in all of New York City. Everyone knows that.

"But would you like to eat gefilte fish," Harry asked, "if the fish was a friend of yours?"

Papa stood absolutely still right in the middle of the sidewalk. "Harry," he said, "Harry, what have you done to Mama's fish?"

"Leah did it too," Harry said.

Papa turned to me. Putting his hands on my shoulders, he looked right into my eyes. Papa's brown eyes were not large, but they were very bright. Most of the time his eyes smiled at us, but when he was angry or upset, like now, they could cut us like knives. "Leah," he said, "what did you do to Mama's fish?"

"Please, Papa," I said, "don't let Mama kill our fish. His name is Joe. We love him, and we want to keep him for a pet."

114

"Where is he now?" Papa asked.

I looked down at my hands and began to pick my fingernail. I didn't want to tell Papa where Joe was. But he put his hand on my chin and forced my face up. "Where's the fish now?" he asked again. His voice was gentle but those eyes were cutting me up.

"In Mrs. Ginzburg's bathtub," I mumbled.

Papa started walking again, faster now. We trailed along behind him, not holding his hands anymore. He didn't say anything for a while. But when we got to our front stoop, he stopped to talk to us. "We are going to Mrs. Ginzburg's apartment and we are getting that fish," he said. "It's your mother's fish and it cost her a lot of money. She had to save a little out of what I give her each week just so she could buy such a big fish and make an extra nice Passover holiday for all of us." When we got to Mrs. Ginzburg's, Papa said to her, "We've come to take the fish home. I'm sorry for the trouble."

"Oh, he was not trouble," Mrs. Ginzburg said.

"Well, he would have been, as soon as you wanted to take a bath," Papa said.

We didn't say anything.

Mrs. Ginzburg let the water out of the tub. Papa didn't need a strainer to catch Joe. He just used his hands and the bucket.

It was much easier going back upstairs than it had been coming down. Papa carried the bucket. I ran the water, and without any ceremony Papa poured Joe in. He flitted through the water so gaily you'd think he was happy to be home. Foolish Joe.

"Carp are for eating," Papa said, "just like chicken. You always eat two helpings of chicken."

"We never met the chicken," I said.

Papa shook his head. "That's not the point, Leah. What God put on this earth to eat, we eat. We don't kill more creatures than we need, and we don't kill them for fun, but we eat what must be eaten. It would break Mama's heart if she realized you children didn't like to eat her gefilte fish. We won't tell her about any of this. Mrs. Ginzburg won't tell her either."

So nobody told Mama about how we had stolen her carp. Luckily, I was at school when she made Joe into gefilte fish. When I got home I asked Harry how he could have stood watching her catch Joe with her strainer and carry him off into the kitchen.

"I didn't watch," Harry said. "When I saw her go for that strainer and her club, I went right down to Mrs. Ginzburg's. But even there I could smell fish cooking."

Although Mama opened all the windows that afternoon, and no one else seemed to notice anything, Harry and I thought we smelled fish cooking for days.

We cried ourselves to sleep that night, and the next night too. Then we made ourselves stop crying. After that, we felt as if we were years older than Mama and Papa.

One night about a week after Passover, though, we were sitting in the kitchen helping Mama shell peas when Papa came home. As he walked through the door, we noticed that he was carrying something orange and black and white and furry in his arms. It was a beautiful big tri-color cat.

"They had too many cats hanging around the loft," Papa said. "This one seemed so friendly and pretty that I brought her home."

Mama seemed surprised, but she let the cat stay. She was a clean cat, and good at chasing the rats out of our kitchen. We called her Joe. Mama couldn't understand that.

I'm an old lady now — a grandmother, as a matter of fact. My daughters buy gefilte fish in jars at the supermarket. They think their uncle Harry and I don't eat it because it isn't as good as the kind our mother made. We don't tell them that we never ate Mama's either.

Pesah Pillow Placecards

We recline on pillows at the seder because rest is a privilege of the free. Here's how to create puffy placecards for those inclined to recline. This is a cooperative family craft and a special souvenir for your seder guests.

9 x 12–inch sheets of felt
   (2 per placecard)
Craft glue
Extra sheets of felt for
   decorative designing
Thin-point permanent
   markers in assorted colors
Optional: rickrack, seam
   binding, sequins, and the
   like
Batting to use for stuffing

Glue together three sides of two felt sheets to form a pillow-case. When it's completely dry, stuff the case with batting, then close the remaining side with glue. You now have a mini-pillow ready for surface decoration. Be sure to write with permanent marker each guest and/or family member's name on his or her pillow. Add spring or Pesah-theme felt cutouts by gluing them directly onto the pillow. Felt cutouts can include Kiddush cup, matzah, pyramids and palm trees, a baby in a basket, bulrushes, frogs, parsley, flowers, a shank bone, bricks and mortar, an egg, Moses with a staff, the Red Sea, and more — use your "Pesah imagination"! Rickrack, sequins, and the like can be added visuals for zippy embellishment. Place the pillows, name side up, on your dining room chairs, and you're ready to answer the four questions in style!

Haroset

Cleaning the house and changing dishes tells you that Passover is near but when you make haroset, *you know the holiday has arrived.*

½ cup shelled walnuts

3 large apples

¼ cup sweet red wine or grape juice

1 teaspoon cinnamon

Put the walnuts in a large bowl. Quarter and core the apples. Grind, chop, or blend the nuts and apples until they have the consistency of chunky peanut butter. Stir in a little wine at a time until the mixture becomes like applesauce. Add the cinnamon, and refrigerate. *Haroset* tastes better when it is at least a day old, so it should be made the day before the seder.

The Onomatopoeic "Had Gadya"

Here is a fun way for your family to sing the cumulative song "Had Gadya," which means "One Only Kid" (as in baby goat). Ask each seder participant to be one of the animals or objects mentioned in the song. Instruct the participants that when their animal or object is mentioned, they should make the appropriate sound. It will go something like this:

Had gadya, had gadya	
That my father bought for two *zuzim* [coins],	*Clink, clink*
Had gadya, had gadya.	
Then came a cat	*Meow*
That ate the kid	*Baaaaa*
That my father bought for two *zuzim,*	*Clink, clink*
Had gadya, had gadya.	
Then came a dog	*Woof, woof*
That bit the cat	*Meow*
That ate the kid	*Baaaaa*
That my father bought for two *zuzim,*	*Clink, clink*
Had gadya, had gadya	
Then came a stick	*(Hit the table)*
That beat the dog	*Woof, woof*
That bit the cat	*Meow*
That ate the kid	*Baaaaa*
That my father bought for two *zuzim,*	*Clink, clink*
Had gadya, had gadya.	
Then came a fire	*Woooooooooo*
That burned the stick . . .	*(Hit the table)*

Then came some water	*Ssssssssss*
That quenched the fire . . .	*Woooooooooo*
Then came an ox	*Ugh, ugh*
That drank the water . . .	*Ssssssssss*
Then came the butcher	*(Make a chopping motion)*
Who slaughtered the ox . . .	*Ugh, ugh*
Then came the angel of death	*Whoosh*
Who killed the butcher . . .	*(Make a chopping motion)*
Then came the Holy One	*(Silence)*
Who killed the angel of death	*Whoosh*
Who killed the butcher	*(Make a chopping motion)*
Who slaughtered the ox	*Ugh, ugh*
That drank the water	*Ssssssssss*
That quenched the fire	*Woooooooooo*
That burned the stick	*(Hit the table)*
That beat the dog	*Woof, woof*
That bit the cat	*Meow*
That ate the kid	*Baaaaa*
That my father bought for two *zuzim,*	*Clink, clink*
Had gadya, had gadya.	

121

Shavuot

The Giving of the Torah

Shavuot, the Feast of Weeks, takes place exactly seven weeks after Passover. Seven is a powerful, indivisible number suggesting completion. Although it is not well known, Shavuot is a holiday of tremendous importance. During Passover the Jews broke free from slavery, but they needed more than that. They needed to know how to live good lives before they could become complete human beings.

Shavuot celebrates the event that gave the people the direction they needed, God's instruction to the Jews at Mount Sinai. To make sure there would be no misunderstanding, God spoke to everyone — all six hundred thousand Jews — at the same time. God gave them the Torah, including the Ten Commandments, which told them how to behave. There are actually 613 very specific commandments in the Torah. The Ten Commandments include all these commandments in a general way. Another name for Shavuot is Zeman Mattan Torahtenu, the Time of the Giving of Our Torah.

Since the Torah, which gives nourishment to the spirit, is often likened to milk and honey, eating cheese, fruit, honey, and wheat (because of the *omer*) is a tasty part of Shavuot. Blintzes are traditional because they are made of wheat flour, cheese, and sometimes fruit. Because Shavuot also celebrates the harvest of the first fruits, people fill the synagogue and home with green branches and flowers. Some synagogues have grass on the floor during the special services of Shavuot, because Jews stood on grass when they received the Torah.

The 613 Commandments

Music and lyrics by Debbie Friedman
Abridged Version

CHORUS

Well, there were six hun-dred and thir-teen com-mand-ments that Mo-ses hand-ed to us. ___ As we stood at the foot of the moun-tain of Si-nai, our dear Mo-ses start-ed to fuss. ___ He threw two tab-lets ___ on-to the ground, ___ And much to our sur-prise, The ten com-mand-ments broke in-to pie-ces, and we could-n't be-lieve ___ our ___ eyes. ___

VERSE

___ Be-cause the To-rah was much too long ___ to de-scribe to all the Jews, ___ Our God de-cid-ed to write ___ ___ ten com-mand-ments that said the dont's ___ and do's. ___ Ev-ery com-mand-ment talked a-bout ___ the way we had ___ to ___ live When we work or play, ___ cook or clean, ___ bor-row, take, ___ or give.

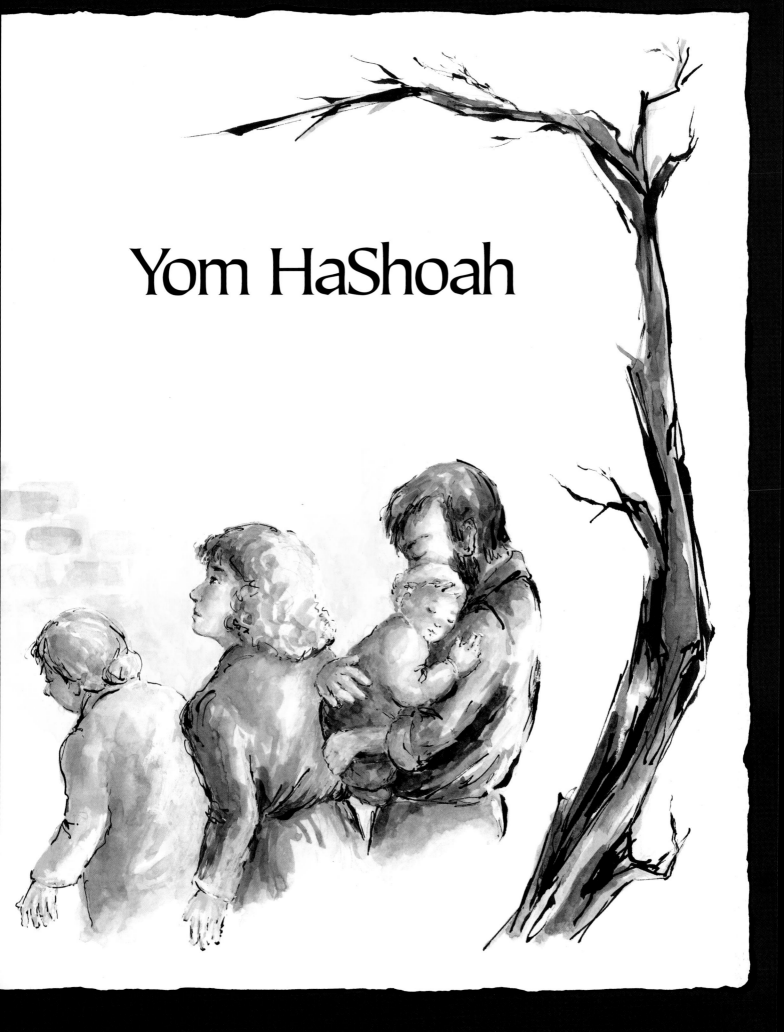

Yom HaShoah

Yom HaShoah

Holocaust Remembrance Day

A terrible event doesn't always end when the moment passes, because every time we remember what happened, we relive the pain. To avoid suffering again, some people refuse to speak of or listen to anything that reminds them of the past. Learning about the Holocaust, the murder of six million Jews in Europe during World War II, is shocking and disturbing. It's natural to avoid pain, but we need to know history. The victims deserve to be remembered, no matter how distressing it is for us: our memory preserves their lives. We also owe it to ourselves. By understanding what happened when the world allowed intolerance and hatred, perhaps we can prevent its tragic conclusion from happening again.

From 1939 to 1945, a man named Adolf Hitler and his followers, members of Germany's National Socialist party, or Nazis for short, tried to make Germany the ruling country of the world. They crushed any individual or nation that attempted to stop them. With armed soldiers and tanks, the Nazis invaded nearly every country in Europe and used brutal force to make nations accept German rule.

In addition to his plan to conquer the world, Hitler burned with another passion: he wanted to eliminate Jews from the human race. He had no reason, except that he regarded them as "inferior." If only one person had wanted to commit this act of genocide, the destruction of a people, it would have simply been a mad and vicious idea. But Hitler, a cunning and ambitious politician, was a genius at spreading hatred and fear.

Hitler told the Germans that the Jews were responsible for their having lost World War I. He also blamed them for destroying the economy, for being disloyal to Germany despite their distinguished military service in previous wars, and for weakening the pure, or Aryan, German race through intermarriage.

Although Germany had started World War I in 1914, by 1918 it had lost the war. The defeat humiliated the country and destroyed its economy. When Hitler came to power in 1933, the Germans were hungry, out of work, and desperate for help. He promised his people that they would rise again, because they were a "superior" race, but the only way for this to happen was to get rid of the Jews.

Imagine if today a political leader said that the way to make America stronger was to throw out African-Americans, Asians, or Latinos. Most people would shake their heads at the absurdity of the idea, a few might laugh, but some might listen. That's what happened in Germany. The educated people didn't pay much attention at first, and by the time they did, Hitler had the support of the masses.

Hitler's anti-Jewish propaganda wasn't new. For over a thousand years, Jews had suffered persecution in Europe. Sometimes it meant that Jews had to live in a certain quarter of the city, and couldn't attend the university, own land, or practice certain professions. At other times Jews were forced to convert to Christianity or be killed. In Eastern Europe, pogroms, or campaigns of random destruction, beatings, and killings in Jewish villages, were common.

The Nazis ultimately took anti-Semitism to a new, unimaginable degree. They began gradually, by passing laws that required Jews to wear yellow Stars of David on their clothing, prohibited them from going to school, and did not allow them to travel after dark. Later, Jews were rounded up and sent to ghettos or camps, or were killed outright.

Hitler took his message of hate to Holland, Belgium, France, Italy, Yugoslavia, Hungary, Czechoslovakia, Romania, Russia, and Poland. The Nazis needed the cooperation of local people to find Jews, and in every country some people helped the Nazis deport Jews. Without these collaborators, Hitler never could have killed so many. By the war's end, six million Jews had died, two-thirds of the total population of European Jews.

The Nazis employed the highest technology of the time to accomplish their appalling crime. They built concentration camps for slave labor and death camps where people were gassed to death and their bodies were burned in ovens. Most of the death camps were in Eastern Europe, because the Nazis regarded Poles and other Eastern Europeans as racially inferior, and the Germans didn't care what those people thought about the odor of burning bodies. *Holocaust* means burnt sacrifice.

There was little the Jews could do to save themselves. By separating the Jews from the rest of the population and taking away their property, jobs, and businesses, the Nazis made the Jews outcasts. They were no longer citizens of the countries in which they had lived for centuries. When the Jews of Europe asked the world to help them, there was little response; without a government of their own to protect them, the Jews were powerless.

Many Jews found ways to fight back, however. Some worked in underground movements throughout Europe to defeat the Nazis. Jews in slave labor camps sabotaged the Nazis by producing shoddy goods on purpose. In April 1943, when the Jews in the Warsaw Ghetto learned that the Nazis were about to kill every Jew there, they did not go meekly. Although they knew they would lose, they used their last strength to fight for their honor and dignity.

The Holocaust didn't happen thousands of years ago. There are people living today who experienced it. There are films of the concentration camps. Because it is so real and so close to our own time, we wonder: could it happen here? We also struggle to imagine how such a horrible event could happen. No one stopped it, not even God. Jewish holidays celebrate the stories of God's protection. The Holocaust forces us to think about God's silence.

Immediately after the war, many Jews couldn't bear to think of a holiday commemorating the Holocaust, but others said, "We must never forget." They wanted a day set aside to remember the murdered six million. After years of debate, the Israeli government set the twenty-seventh of Nisan as Yom HaShoah, literally, the Day of the Total Destruction. Even the date was controversial. Religious Jews felt it was too close to Passover, a joyful holiday, and would diminish Passover's celebration. They wanted it later. But others wanted it to come close to and before Yom Ha'atzmaut, the celebration of

Israel becoming a Jewish homeland. They believed the holidays belonged together because the creation of Israel was a response to the Holocaust.

Because Yom HaShoah is a modern holiday, what it misses in tradition it makes up for in creativity. Some people use a plain clay cup, a symbol of poverty, instead of a silver cup to bless the wine. Some people fast; others eat only tasteless food. Congregations have created special services to mark the day, including the recital of the memorial prayer for the dead. In Israel, on the eve of the holiday, a siren whines over the entire country to remind Israelis to stop whatever they are doing and to take a moment to remember.

Unlike other holidays like Passover, when we eat matzah, or Sukkot, when we build little huts, the Holocaust cannot be reenacted. On Yom HaShoah we remember the Holocaust and try to imagine the rage, fear, and pain of the lost Jews of Europe. We also remember the few who risked their lives to save their Jewish neighbors.

Poems from Terezinstadt

Terezinstadt was a concentration camp near Prague, Czechoslovakia, that the Nazis built in 1941. Like all the concentration camps, it caused terrible suffering for its occupants: they were starved, overcrowded, ill, and forced to do slave labor.

During the four years of its operation, fifteen thousand children lived there. Only one hundred returned home after the war. The children lived together, which made them less lonely and frightened. The teachers in charge of the children were often people who had opposed the Nazis, and for that reason they were imprisoned.

The teachers secretly taught the children and encouraged them to paint, write, and perform puppet shows. Even though most of the children died, they left their words and pictures to help us remember their gifts and their suffering.

AT TEREZIN

When a new child comes
Everything seems strange to him.
What, on the ground I have to lie?
Eat black potatoes? No! Not I!
I've got to stay? It's dirty here!
The floor — why, look, it's dirt, I fear!
And I'm supposed to sleep on it?
I'll get all dirty!

Here the sound of shouting, cries,
And oh, so many flies.
Everyone knows flies carry disease.
Oooh, something bit me! Wasn't that a bedbug?
Here in Terezín, life is hell
And when I'll go home again, I can't yet tell.

"Teddy," Barrack L 410, 1943

HOMESICK

I've lived in the ghetto here more than a year,
In Terezín, in the black town now,
And when I remember my old home so dear,
I can love it more than I did, somehow.

Ah, home, home,
Why did they tear me away?
Here the weak die easy as a feather
And when they die, they die forever.

I'd like to go back home again,
It makes me think of sweet spring flowers.
Before, when I used to live at home,
It never seemed so dear and fair.

I remember now those golden days . . .
But maybe I'll be going there soon again.

People walk along the street,
You see at once on each you meet
That there's a ghetto here,
A place of evil and of fear.
There's little to eat and much to want,
Where bit by bit, it's horror to live.
But no one must give up!
The world turns and times change.

Yet we all hope the time will come
When we'll go home again.
Now I know how dear it is
And often I remember it.

        Anonymous, Barrack 9.3, 1943

ON A SUMMER EVENING

On a purple, sun-shot evening
Under wide-flowering chestnut trees
Upon the threshold full of dust
Yesterday, today, the days are all like these.

Trees flower forth in beauty,
Lovely too their very wood all gnarled and old
That I am half afraid to peer
Into their crowns of green and gold.

The sun has made a veil of gold
So lovely that my body aches.
Above, the heavens shriek with blue
Convinced I've smiled by some mistake.
The world's abloom and seems to smile.
I want to fly but where, how high?
If in barbed wire, things can bloom
Why couldn't I? I will not die!

        The children in Barracks L 318 and L 417,
            ages ten to sixteen, 1944

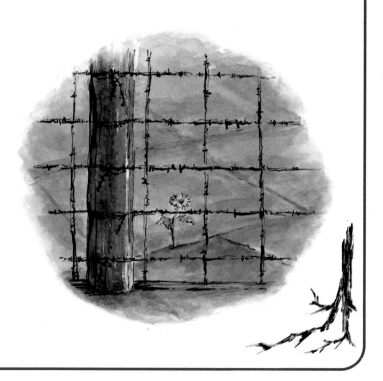

Rescuers

The Nazis hid the enormity of their atrocities from the outside world. Non-Jews weren't allowed to visit the disease-filled, crowded ghettos the Jews were forced to live in, nor did civilians see the camps. Most of the world didn't know that millions of Jews were suffering starvation, firing squads, or gas chambers, because almost no one wanted to know. But a few people did pay attention, and they couldn't ignore the pain of others. They risked their lives, and their children's lives, to save Jews. These few good people rescued most of the five hundred thousand Jews who survived the war.

Alex and Mela Roslan were two of those rescuers. They were living in Warsaw with their two children, Yorek, age eleven, and Marishka, age eight, when the Nazis invaded Poland. Even though they were poor and struggled to find enough food for themselves — and even though the Nazis had erected signs all over Warsaw that said, "Anyone caught hiding a Jew will be immediately put to death, along with his family!" — when they were asked to hide eight-year-old Jacob, they didn't hesitate. Soon they were hiding not only Jacob but his two younger brothers as well.

Alex built a hiding place for the boys under the kitchen sink, but because the Nazis offered a reward to Poles who turned in Jews, the apartment was searched and the boys nearly found. For this reason, the Roslans were forced to move throughout the war. Jacob and his youngest brother, David, survived the war, but Sholom was too sick by the time he moved to the Roslans' home to live more than a few months. Yorek also died, in 1944, having been shot by a German soldier.

After the war, the Roslans discovered that the brothers' father had survived and was living in Israel, so the boys left the Roslans. Today Jacob and David are scientists in Israel with families of their own. Because Alex and Mela, who moved to the United States after the boys left, still feel like parents to Jacob and David, they have remained close with frequent calls, letters, and visits.

Six Tulips

Because so many Dutch people rescued Jews during the Holocaust, putting six yellow tulips in a vase on Yom HaShoah is a reminder of the worst and best that people do.

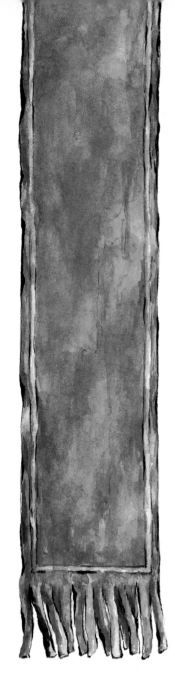

Anne Frank

Anne Frank was thirteen years old in 1942, when she and her family went into hiding in Amsterdam. She kept a diary, which was given to her on her birthday and which she named Kitty, from the beginning of her time in the hidden room until her family was betrayed and deported to Auschwitz, a death camp in Poland, on August 4, 1944. Anne, her sister, Margot, and their mother, Edith, died in Bergen-Belsen, another camp. Only Anne's father, Otto, survived.

Miep Gies, a friend of the Franks who brought them food and clothing while they were in hiding, found Anne's diary by her bed and saved it. When Otto Frank returned to Holland, Miep gave him the diary, which was all that remained of his family. In 1947, a friend persuaded Frank to publish the diary under the title The Annex, *Anne's name for the hiding place. Her eloquent account of the war as a young person in hiding gave a voice and face to all those who suffered Nazi persecution. The house she hid in is now a historical landmark in Amsterdam where visitors from all over the world come to imagine what life in hiding was like for Anne Frank and her family.*

Friday, 21 August, 1942

DEAR KITTY,

The entrance to our hiding place has now been properly concealed. Mr. Kraler thought it would be better to put a cupboard in front of our door (because a lot of houses are being searched for hidden bicycles), but of course it had to be a movable cupboard that can open like a door.

Mr. Vossen made the whole thing. We had already let him into the secret and he can't do enough to help. If we want to go downstairs, we have to first bend down and then jump, because the step has gone. The first three days we were all going about with masses of lumps on our foreheads, because we all knocked ourselves against the low doorway. Now we have nailed a cloth filled with wood wool against the top of the door. Let's see if that helps!

I'm not working much at present; I'm giving myself holidays until September. Then Daddy is going to give me lessons; it's shocking how much I've forgotten already. There is little change in our life here. Mr. Van Daan and I usually manage to upset each other, it's just the opposite with Margot whom he likes very much. Mummy sometimes treats me just like a baby, which I can't bear. Otherwise things are going better. I still don't like Peter any more, he is so boring; he flops lazily on his bed half the time, does a bit of carpentry, and then goes back for another snooze. What a fool!

It is lovely weather and in spite of everything we make the most we can of it by lying on a camp bed in the attic, where the sun shines through an open window.

Yours, Anne

Friday, 9 October, 1942

Dear Kitty,

I've only got dismal and depressing news for you today. Our many Jewish friends are being taken away by the dozen. These people are treated by the Gestapo without a shred of decency, being loaded into cattle trucks and sent to Westerbork, the big Jewish camp in Drente. Westerbork sounds terrible: only one washing cubicle for a hundred people and not nearly enough lavatories. There is no separate accommodation. Men, women, and children all sleep together. One hears of frightful immorality because of this; and a lot of the women, and even girls, who stay there any length of time are expecting babies.

It is impossible to escape; most of the people in the camp are branded as inmates by their shaven heads and many also by their Jewish appearance.

If it is as bad as this in Holland whatever will it be like in the distant and barbarous regions they are sent to? We assume that most of them are murdered. The English radio speaks of their being gassed.

Perhaps this is the quickest way to die. I feel terribly upset. I couldn't tear myself away while Miep told these dreadful stories; and she herself was equally wound up for that matter. Just recently, for instance, a poor old crippled Jewess was sitting on her doorstep; she had been told to wait there by the Gestapo, who had gone to fetch a car to take her away. The poor old thing was terrified by the guns that were shooting at English planes overhead, and by the glaring beams of the searchlights. But Miep did not dare take her in; no one would undergo such a risk. The Germans strike without the slightest mercy. Elli too is very quiet: her boyfriend has got to go to Germany. She is afraid that the airmen who fly over our homes will drop their bombs, often weighing a million kilos, on Dirk's head. Jokes such as "he's not likely to get a million" and "it only takes one bomb" are in rather bad taste. Dirk is certainly not the only one who has to go: trainloads of boys leave daily. If they stop at a small station en route, sometimes some of them manage to get out unnoticed and escape; perhaps a few manage it. This, however, is not the end of my bad news. Have you ever heard of hostages? That's the latest thing in penalties for sabotage. Can you imagine anything so dreadful?

Prominent citizens — innocent people — are thrown into prison to await their fate. If the saboteur can't be traced, the Gestapo simply put about five hostages against the wall. Announcements of their deaths appear in the papers frequently. These outrages are described as "fatal accidents." Nice people, the Germans! To think that I was once one of them too! No, Hitler took away our nationality long ago. In fact, Germans and Jews are the greatest enemies in the world.

Yours, Anne

Thursday, 25 May, 1944

Dear Kitty,

There's something fresh every day. This morning our vegetable man was picked up for having two Jews in his house. It's a great blow to us, not only that those poor Jews are balancing on the edge of an abyss, but it's terrible for the man himself.

The world has turned topsy-turvy, respectable people are being sent off to concentration camps, prisons, and lonely cells, and the dregs that remain govern young and old, rich and poor. One person walks into the trap through the black market, a second through helping the Jews or other people who've had to go "underground"; anyone who isn't a member of the N.S.B. [National Socialist Party] doesn't know what may happen to him from one day to another.

136

This man is a great loss to us too. The girls can't and aren't allowed to haul along our share of potatoes, so the only thing to do is to eat less. I will tell you how we shall do that; it's certainly not going to make things any pleasanter. Mummy says we shall cut out breakfast altogether, have porridge and bread for lunch, and for supper fried potatoes and possibly once or twice per week vegetables or lettuce, nothing more. We're going to be hungry, but anything is better than being discovered.

Yours, Anne

Friday, 21 July, 1944

Dear Kitty,

Now I am getting really hopeful, now things are going well at last. Yes, really, they're going well! Super news! An attempt has been made on Hitler's life and not even by Jewish communists or English capitalists this time, but by a proud German general, and what's more, he's a count, and still quite young. The Führer's life was saved by Divine Providence and, unfortunately, he managed to get off with just a few scratches and burns. A few officers and generals who were with him have been killed and wounded. The chief culprit was shot.

Anyway, it certainly shows that there are lots of officers and generals who are sick of the war and would like to see Hitler descend into a bottomless pit.

When they've disposed of Hitler, their aim is to establish a military dictator, who will make peace with the Allies, then they intend to rearm and start another war in about twenty years' time. Perhaps the Divine Power tarried on purpose in getting him out of the way, because it would be much easier and more advantageous to the Allies if the impeccable Germans kill each other off; it'll make less work for the Russians and the English and they'll be able to begin rebuilding their own towns all the sooner.

But still, we're not that far yet, and I don't want to anticipate the glorious events too soon. Still, you must have noticed, this is all sober reality and that I'm in quite a matter-of-fact mood today; for once, I'm not jabbering about high ideals. And what's more, Hitler has even been so kind as to announce to his faithful, devoted people that from now on everyone in the armed forces must obey the Gestapo, and that any soldier who knows that one of his superiors was involved in this low, cowardly attempt upon his life may shoot the same on the spot, without court-martial.

What a perfect shambles it's going to be. Little Johnnie's feet begin hurting him during a long march, he's snapped at by his boss, the officer, Johnnie grabs his rifle and cries out: "You wanted to murder the Führer, so there's your reward." One bang and the proud chief who dared to tick off little Johnnie has passed into eternal life (or is it eternal death?). In the end, whenever an officer finds himself up against a soldier, or having to take the lead, he'll be wetting his pants from anxiety, because the soldiers will dare to say more than they do. Do you gather a bit what I mean, or have I been skipping too much from one subject to another? I can't help it; the prospect that I may be sitting on school benches next October makes me feel far too cheerful to be logical! Oh, dearie me, hadn't I just told you that I didn't want to be too hopeful? Forgive me, they haven't given me the name "little bundle of contradictions" all for nothing!

Yours, Anne

On August 14, 1944, all the occupants of the Annex were arrested and sent to German and Dutch concentration camps. In March 1945, two months before Holland was liberated, Anne died in the concentration camp at Bergen-Belsen.

A Visit to the United States
Holocaust Memorial Museum

In April 1993, the United States Holocaust Memorial Museum opened in Washington, D.C. Visitors can experience the Holocaust by walking through a barrack from a concentration camp, watching survivors tell their stories on video, and viewing photos and artifacts such as a Danish fishing boat that took Jews to safety. One wall of the museum is covered with tiles decorated by children who were asked to sum up their feelings about the Holocaust. The next time your family visits the nation's capital, you too can stop at the museum to gain a better understanding of this horrific event. Then you may be inspired to create your own "plaque of remembrance."

Menorah

Many people light candles on Yom HaShoah, because candles are always lit when someone dies and on the anniversary of a death. Candles are also part of life: we light them on Shabbat to celebrate the Creation.

To remember the six million, light six candles. Here is a simple menorah you can make in the shape of a Star of David. During the war, Jews were forced to wear yellow cloth Stars of David on their clothes so they could be identified easily.

You need six tongue depressors, at least three quarters of an inch wide. Glue three pieces in a triangle, so that you have two triangles. Glue the triangles together to make a Star of David. In each corner, glue a bottle cap. Melt the bottom of a Shabbat candle, and put one in each corner.

Eili, Eili
(My God, My God)
by Hannah Senesh

Hannah Senesh was a young Hungarian Jew who escaped to Palestine during the war and joined others working to bring Jews out of Europe. After parachuting into Yugoslavia in 1944, she returned to Hungary, where she was captured, tortured, and killed by the Nazis. The following poem is taken from her private writings.

> *My God, my God,*
> *I pray that these things never end:*
> *The sand and the sea,*
> *The rush of the waters,*
> *The crash of the heavens,*
> *The prayer of the heart.*
> *The sand and the sea,*
> *The rush of the waters,*
> *The crash of the heavens,*
> *The prayer of the heart.*

Yom Ha'atzmaut

Yom Ha'atzmaut

Israeli Independence Day

The Holocaust convinced the Jewish people that they needed their own country. Many Jews believed that the Holocaust would not have happened if they had been able to get out of Europe. Because they didn't have a government to fight Hitler nor a country to take refuge in, they were helpless.

Jews first settled in Israel three thousand years ago, but few Jews remained after the Romans drove them out in 70 C.E. For the next two thousand years, then, the Jews were without a country. For brief periods during that time, they were welcome in other countries, but most of their history consisted of prejudice and persecution. In Russia and Poland, Jews suffered pogroms, and in other parts of Eastern Europe they were accused of causing plagues and using human blood for religious ceremonies. Because of these experiences, and because they always believed that Israel was a special place, the land of their ancestors, Jews always prayed for the time when they would return to Israel. At Passover the seder ends with the fond wish, "Next year in Jerusalem!"

Roughly one hundred years ago, European Jews began to return to Palestine, the name for Israel then, with the dream of having a country again. They were tired of being picked on, of not being allowed to own land or get good jobs, and they were always afraid of being beaten up. In 1897, a young writer in Vienna named Theodore Herzl called a meeting of Jews from all over the world to plan the birth of a new Jewish state. At this meeting the World Zionist Organization began Zionism, the movement to build a Jewish homeland (Zion is an ancient name for Israel). Herzl's words "If you will it, it is no dream" became the Zionist slogan, and even though Herzl had never lived in Israel, he became known as the Father of Zionism. Herzl's writings moved a whole generation of Jews to do more than dream and pray. They inspired people to act.

The early pioneers were tough. They had to be. The land was either desert or swamp, and these young people weren't used to working in the fields. But the idea of a country where Jews had the freedom to be anything — leaders, farmers, police officers, taxi drivers, and teachers — kept them working hard to make the dream come true.

Still, they had problems besides tender hands and hard earth. The Turks, who ruled Palestine, had no intention of allowing a Jewish state, and the surrounding Arab countries didn't welcome the new settlers, either. When Great Britain took over Palestine from the Turks in 1920, the Jewish pioneers became hopeful. In the Balfour Declaration, the British promised the Jews that one day they would have their own state, just as the British had already created Syria, Lebanon, Iraq, and Jordan for the Arabs.

When Hitler came to power, thousands of European Jews tried to flee to Palestine, but the British would only allow in a few. At the war's end, most of the Jews who survived wanted to leave Europe and begin a new life in Palestine. Still, the British wouldn't allow them in, fearing that the neighboring Arab countries would protest.

The United Nations solved the problem by cutting Palestine in half, giving half to the Jews and the other half to the Arabs. The Jews agreed, but the Arabs wanted all of Palestine. They went to war, and despite the British helping the Arabs, the Jews won. On May 14, 1948, the British left Palestine and the country was reborn as the State of Israel, the first Jewish state in nineteen hundred years.

Like Yom HaShoah, Yom Ha'atzmaut is a new holiday. It began the day Israel became a country, and it celebrates not only independence but the spirit of the people. Many of those who fought for independence were young people who had survived the Holocaust. They hadn't given up; they still believed life was worth fighting for. Israel's national anthem is called "HaTikvah," which means "The Hope." Because they never gave up hope, the Jewish people returned to their ancient land as a free people.

Yom Ha'atzmaut in Israel is like the Fourth of July in America — a time for picnics, barbecues, and noisy fun. When the holiday begins at sundown, bonfires light the surrounding hills. People sing songs about modern Israel around a campfire, and there are bands and dancing in the city parks.

During the day, instead of fireworks exploding in the sky, Israeli air force jets do daring aerial feats with parachutists. But Israelis do more than watch the sky on Yom Ha'atzmaut. They play soccer, march in parades, and watch a major Bible quiz on TV. Children from all over the world compete in this contest. For Israeli students, the Bible is not just a religious book but the history of their country.

In America, Yom Ha'atzmaut is a day to tighten the connection between Israeli and American Jews. In New York, thousands march in the Israel Day parade waving Israeli flags, singing songs, and eating falafel.

HaTikvah
(The Hope)

N. H. Imber

With dignity

Kol__ ōd ba-lé-vav p' - ni - ma ne-fesh Y'-hu-di hō - mi - ya ul'-

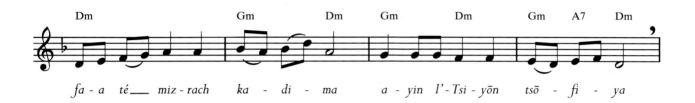

fa-a té__ miz-rach ka-di-ma a - yin l'-Tsi-yōn tsō - fi - ya

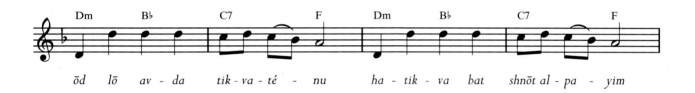

ōd lō av-da tik-va-té-nu ha-tik-va bat shnōt al-pa-yim

li - yōt am chof-shi b'-ar-tsé-nu e - rets Tsi-yōn Y'-ru-sha-la - yim

li - yōt am chof-shi b'-ar-tsé-nu e - rets Tsi-yōn Y'-ru-sha-la - yim.

As long as a Jewish heart beats,
and as long as Jewish eyes look eastward,
then our two-thousand-year hope
to be a free nation in Zion is not dead.

A Trip to Israel

A Few Facts

Israel is six thousand miles from New York City. It's small, about the size of Massachusetts. Its weather is warm and dry, as in Los Angeles, and it rains in the winter. Israel has lots of sun, some snow, deserts, and forest. Four million people live there. Three million, six hundred thousand are Jews; 615,000 are Muslim Arabs; and 102,000 are Christians.

Israel's history runs deep. Underneath the earth upon which it stands are layers rich with thousands of years of broken pieces of pottery, glass, and bones. But there is also a lot of history to see above ground. You can visit the places the Bible describes: the Red Sea the Israelites crossed, the wall of the Great Temple in Jerusalem, or the trees planted long ago by the Jewish National Fund, when Israel was only a hope, not yet a reality.

Jerusalem

Israel has three major cities: Haifa, Tel Aviv, and Jerusalem. The first two are like busy modern cities anywhere — lots of people, tall buildings, and traffic. But Jerusalem has that and more. Jews, Christians, and Muslims all call Jerusalem their special city, and perhaps that's why such a variety of people live there. As you walk down the street, you might see nuns speaking Hebrew, a Bedouin Arab walking with his camel, a soldier sitting with a gun across his lap, two men in long black coats and black hats, and vendors selling delicious rolls or fruit juice.

Jerusalem is where the Great Temple was built twenty-seven hundred years ago. All that's left of it is the Western Wall. Many people pray there and leave messages for God between the stones of the wall. Five hundred years ago, the Turks built a huge stone wall to surround what is now called the Old City. Mixed in with these old stones are ancient buildings, pizza places, museums, zoos, movie theaters, and synagogues.

Israelis

People who are born in Israel call themselves *sabras*, after the cactus fruit that grows naturally there. The fruit is prickly on the outside and sweet on the inside. Israelis aren't always polite or hesitant to express their opinions, but if you're lost on a street corner or need a ride, someone will stop to help. Since Israel is open to any Jew who wishes to move there, there are always lots of newcomers in the country. In the last few years, tens of thousands of Jews have emigrated from Russia and Ethiopia. The Israeli government helps recent immigrants by giving them a place to live, Hebrew lessons, and assistance in finding work. But it is the *sabra* who helps the newly arriving people feel that they are part of a big family.

Growing Up in Israel

Because Israel is a small, poor country and everyone is always busy just trying to make life work, Israeli kids are very independent. Youngsters grow up quickly and join youth clubs that go hiking and camping. They also are familiar with war. They see soldiers everywhere, hear fighter planes roar overhead, and may have an older brother or sister in the army. Every eighteen-year-old must serve in the army. Living in Israel is not as hard as it was for the first pioneers, but it still takes toughness and patience to live in the small, young country that has too little water and too many enemies.

Why You Can Say *Ice Cream* in Hebrew

There was once a little boy living in Russia who loved Hebrew. The problem was that Hebrew was a dead language, one that hadn't been spoken for two thousand years. But this boy dreamed of the day all Jewish people would once again speak Hebrew. When he grew up, he moved to Israel in 1881 and changed his name to Eliezer Ben-Yehuda.

Ben-Yehuda believed that a people needed not only land but a language of its own. Ben-Yehuda saw that if Israel was to become a modern nation, its three-thousand-year-old language would have to be updated. He made up new words from the roots of the old, wrote a weekly newspaper to introduce the words, and by 1922, Hebrew had grown from seventy-five hundred words to fifty thousand words.

Here are a few common Hebrew words and phrases:

Good morning: *Boker tov*
Thank you: *Todah*
You're welcome: *B'vakashah*
Fish: *Dag*
Dog: *Kelev*
Cat: *Hatoul*
Boy: *Yeled*
Girl: *Yaldah*
Computer: *Mahshav*
Ice Cream: *Glidah*

Brothers

by Shalom Hektin

THE LARGE SHIP WAS ALIVE, overflowing with hundreds of children singing, laughing, and racing the length of the deck.

A small boy stood off to one side, leaning against the rail. He stood motionless, staring at the ocean in the direction from which the ship had come.

"Yosele," a voice called to him. He did not reply. Two girls ran up to him. The one with black braids tugged at his sleeve and said, "Come, Yosele, and join us. Don't be a grouch!" The boy yanked his sleeve from the little girl's friendly grasp and turned away from her to stare again at the sea.

It was March 1943. The passengers of the ship were eight hundred Jewish children who had been rescued from the Nazis. For more than a year they had sailed on dangerous waters, because no country would let them in. At last the good news came — they would be welcomed to their new home, Eretz Israel.

The children had already begun to forget their bitterness, anger, and disappointment when countries had refused to allow them to dock and had forced them to toss about on the seven seas in all sorts of weather. Now they were happy. They were on the Red Sea, and in a day or two they would be in Palestine — their own home.

Only Yosele wasn't happy. At seven, he was the youngest on the ship. He was always alone — dreamy and sad.

Yosele was not the only orphan among the children. Very few were lucky enough to have both, or even one, of their parents. They all had suffered, but little Yosele seemed to suffer more than the others.

150

Maybe it was because he was so young. He had been only four years old when his parents were murdered. Yosele couldn't even remember whether he had a brother or sister. He did remember how his mother had played with him and how she used to hold him in her arms. But how she looked, he couldn't remember. He tried and tried, but couldn't imagine her face.

His father's face wasn't clear, either, but at times it felt to Yosele that his father's tall figure was standing beside him. Yosele seldom laughed. But often, when he fell asleep, he dreamed of his father. Then he would laugh and whisper, "Papa, Papa."

Night covered the countryside and the people of Kibbutz Naan were asleep. Only Dov, the watchman, was awake. He was a young man of twenty-three who had left Poland to come to Palestine five years before. Now Naan was his home. As he stood leaning lightly on his rifle in the dark, his mind drifted back to the Polish village where he'd grown up. He remembered his parents and his little brother.

When Dov had first come to Palestine, he'd wanted to bring his family later. But the war shattered his plans. Now Dov didn't even know where his family was. It had been a long time since he had heard from them.

Dov thought of the hundreds of children who were to pass through the train station near Naan the next day. He was glad so many children had been rescued from death, and like all the others there, he was happy to welcome them. But what of his own family? His little brother? Would he ever find him?

Suddenly, Dov heard a faint rustling nearby, and he smiled. The children of Naan loved him and came often to visit him on the kibbutz. Two shadows crept toward him.

"Who goes there?" he shouted. "Why, you little devils! Don't you know I have the right to shoot you?"

Nine-year-old Amos hung his head in shame, but Yigal retorted, "Go ahead — shoot!" And he slipped into the darkness. Creeping behind Dov, he jumped on his back and teased, "Come on, shoot me, come on, shoot."

After a few moments of wrestling, they all sat down and Dov asked, "Why are you out so late?"

"We couldn't sleep," Yigal said. "Even though we have to be up extra early tomorrow."

"Why?" asked Dov, as though he didn't know.

"Don't you know? Tomorrow morning we're going to the train station to meet the young refugees. All the children here had a secret meeting, and we decided that we have to bring back at least one of the children to live here. At least one, so that we can have a party for the distinguished guest immediately after his arrival in Eretz Israel."

The children looked hopefully at Dov.

"The idea is good," he agreed. "But I don't know whether I can help you. The rescued children are supposed to be taken to one definite place first, and then to be sent to different kibbutzim.

"Come to the station with us. Who knows? Maybe your little brother will be among the children."

Dov's face clouded. Of course he'd go if he knew his brother would be there! But would they even recognize each other? He remained lost in thought, remembering that when he was a boy, people often said he resembled his father.

"Just like his father," Dov suddenly said aloud. He wrinkled his forehead in amazement, but he knew he would go to greet the children tomorrow.

A large crowd had gathered at the station. The children carried white-and-blue banners. Many had boxes filled with oranges and other good things to eat. The desert sun shone in a clear blue sky, and the air was sweet with the fragrance of oranges.

A long train thundered into the station. Laughing children stuck their faces out the train windows. The crowd on the platform roared its welcome.

As soon as the train stopped, the children tumbled out of all parts of it like a gushing sea. Nothing could have stopped them—they had finally come home. Strangers kissed strangers. They began to cry and to laugh, and they were no longer strangers, just one-half of a large family welcoming the other half.

The train was empty, but one child remained. Yosele stared out the window. Suddenly he stiffened. He looked in bewilderment at one face. Then his thin voice cut through the crowd like a razor: "Papa! Papa!"

A shiver went through the crowd as it turned to Yosele. Among the first who ran to the train was Dov. He looked into the lonely face wet with tears. Yosele looked back at the face that had made him cry out, "Papa!" Dov picked him up and suddenly knew. This was his little brother for whom he had yearned all these years.

Dov followed the procession of children returning to Naan. Yosele rested his head on his brother's chest. "What's your name?" Yosele asked.

"Dov or Berl, whichever you want to call me."

"Dov or Berl — not Papa," Yosele said to himself, his face again pained.

Dov pressed the boy closer. Yosele lay against his brother, deep in thought. Then he shook himself as if waking from a dream. He looked around at the generous fields, at the sunny road stretching ahead with thick green bushes framing it. He filled his lungs with clean, fresh air. He watched the children marching to their own music, and he began to sing along.

Slowly, he slid out of Dov's arms, and waving his hand, he ran to join the children. It is difficult to explain why, but Yosele ran directly to the place where the two young friends, Amos and Yigal, were marching side by side. The two boys grasped his hands and held them tight, and they marched together.

Picnic Sheet

Yom Ha'atzmaut comes just at the beginning of the picnic season. Here's a simple idea for a holiday picnic sheet to sit on while you eat falafel sandwiches and think about Israel.

1 single white sheet
6 permanent blue markers
1 permanent blue pen with a
   fine point

Unfold the sheet you're about to make into a gigantic Israeli flag. In the center of the sheet, draw with pencil a large Star of David. The easiest way is to draw two triangles. When you're satisfied with its shape, make broad lines with the blue markers.

Color two horizontal stripes at the top of the sheet and two at the bottom. Now fill in the lines by writing whatever pops into your head about Israel, such as *The people of Israel live; I love falafel; Happy birthday, Israel; Theodore Herzl; Eliezer Ben-Yehuda; Jerusalem; Trees.* This is more fun to do when several of you are working on a different part of the sheet at the same time.

The Star of David

The six-pointed Star of David, also called Magen David or the Shield of David, was believed to have decorated King David's shield and to have magical powers. For hundreds of years it was used by Jews and non-Jews alike. Then, in the nineteenth century, it appeared in synagogue decorations as a symbol of Judaism. At its first meeting in 1897, the World Zionist Organization unfurled a flag combining the star with the blue and white stripes of a *tallit*, or prayer shawl. The Zionist flag became so popular among Jews that it was adopted by Israel when the new country was formed.

154

Falafel

The best food in Israel is the fastest food. Except on Shabbat, Israelis don't spend a lot of time sitting at leisurely meals. Falafel is a delicious fast food, and unlike fries and a burger, it's also good for you. Since this recipe calls for hot oil, be sure to have an adult help you.

1 cup canned chick-peas,
   drained
1 clove garlic
½ teaspoon salt
¼ teaspoon pepper
⅔ cup fine bread crumbs
2 eggs
1 cup oil plus 2 tablespoons

If you have a food processor, mix together the chick-peas, garlic, salt and pepper, and bread crumbs. (If not, use a potato masher to mash the chick-peas, cut the garlic into tiny pieces, and combine the chick-peas, garlic, salt and pepper, and bread crumbs.) Add the eggs and the two tablespoons of oil to the mixture, and mix it well.

Heat the remaining oil in a three-quart pot until the oil begins to bubble. Make the mixture into sixteen balls. With a long-handled slotted spoon, gently put a few balls in the oil. Fry a few at a time until they turn golden brown, about five minutes.

When the falafel balls are cooked, remove them with the spoon and put them on a plate with lots of paper towels to drain the oil. Falafel is great all by itself as a treat, or put a few balls in a piece of pita, or pocket, bread. (It looks like a pancake that opens in the middle.) Add sliced tomatoes and cucumbers. If you can find tahini, a sauce made of sesame seeds, pour it on top, hold the ends of the pita tightly, and dig in!

Shabbat

Shabbat

A Peaceful Island

Shabbat is the best day of the week. It's a day of rest, a day of play, and a day of *No Work!* Not that working is bad. Without it, we wouldn't have houses, food, and families. But sometimes we get carried away with being busy. We forget to take time just to enjoy our lives. Shabbat is a reminder to stop *doing* and relax one day a week.

When did this special day begin? Some people believe it started at the beginning of the world, when God, after making the world in six days, rested on the seventh day.

The Jewish people began to celebrate Shabbat, which means "rest," over three thousand years ago. The Greeks and Romans couldn't understand how resting could be holy, a way to honor God. But the observance of Shabbat may be the most important law in the Torah. By resting on the seventh day, we imitate God and appreciate the work we've done all week.

What is rest? What is work? The Torah offers a hint. First, it gives a detailed description of the work required to build a house of prayer, followed by the commandment to keep the Sabbath. Because these two paragraphs are next to each other, the rabbis decided that anything you have to do to construct a building, including building a fire, is forbidden on the Sabbath.

On Shabbat, no one is supposed to work, including animals. Even the land gets to rest, because we don't even pick a flower on Shabbat. It's the one day human beings don't interfere with the world — we behave as if everything were perfect.

Not doing work is only half of Shabbat. The absence of work allows time for the leisurely moments that make the day a delight. Every *no* allows for a *yes*. Imagine slipping off a backpack full of books and papers on Friday afternoon, knowing you are commanded not even to think about its contents until the following evening. Now you have lots of time to visit friends, play games, and read anything you like.

The laws of Shabbat, which tell you what to do and not to do, make everything you do on that day special — it's the difference between Saturday and Shabbat. The rules take getting used to, but after a while, you begin to look forward to "going" to this peaceful place. Shabbat becomes a home that shelters, warms, and comforts us from the setting of the sun on Friday night until three stars appear in a darkening sky the following evening. The tradition built a day, not a structure, for its people. How many buildings have lasted for three thousand years?

Shabbat begins with lighting two candles. They stand for the opposites in life: light and darkness, holy and profane, work and rest. On Shabbat everything is oneness and harmony. We shift from time being broken into many tasks to time becoming a period of wholeness and completion. Sometimes we feel alone, isolated from others before the start of Shabbat; our interests and concerns keep us separate.

After the candles are lit, the kiddush, the blessing said over wine to proclaim the holiness of the day, is sung. Then, after everyone sips the wine, the hallah, a sweet egg bread, is uncovered for its blessing. Even if the dinner that follows is eaten in the same room as the other meals of the week, it feels special. It's a night when no one is rushed, favorite foods are cooked, and if there is just one night a week for dessert, this is the night.

Shabbat brings the family together — it may be the one meal everyone eats together. School, work, and worries are left behind. The family's change of mood is so dramatic that children may think they have four parents — the two weekday parents, who are sometimes tense, tired, and short-tempered, and the two Shabbat parents, who are cheerful, patient, and relaxed.

Shabbat does more than simply give people a rest. It may be a way to take care of the world. If we all spent one day a week free of pressure and routine, taking time to renew ourselves, celebrating the world's creation and the creative energy that gives life to the world, we might enjoy our lives more and remember how precious life is. A day of rest also gives us the strength to repair the world.

Some people believe that observing Shabbat is as important as working for

nuclear disarmament or environmental conservation. The greeting on Shabbat isn't "Hi" or "Good Morning." It's "*Shabbat shalom,*" which means "May you have a Sabbath of peace."

There is a legend that describes how precious Shabbat is. God said to the Jewish people, "If you follow my laws and accept the Torah, I will give you the most valuable gift I have, the world to come."

"Show us here an example of this world," they asked. So God gave them Shabbat. They didn't have to die to experience a perfect world of peace and harmony. They could have it each week.

Genesis

Adapted from the Torah

Genesis, the name of the first book of the Bible, means the beginning of something coming into being. What you're about to read is from the first words of the Torah. It tells the story of how, according to Jewish tradition, the world got started. Some of the words such as the deep *and a* firmament *are difficult to imagine — maybe because it's impossible to imagine nothingness. Picture the deep as bigger than any hole you've ever seen, and see the firmament as a gigantic arch spanning the world. (*Firmament *means sky or heaven.)*

The Hebrew name for the first book of Torah is Bereshit, which means "in the beginning." Bereshit is the first word of the Torah.

CHAPTER ONE

In the beginning God created the heaven and the earth. Now the earth was unformed and empty, darkness was upon the face of the deep, and the spirit of God hovered over the face of the waters. God said: "Let there be light." And there was light. God saw the light was good, and separated it from the darkness. God called the light Day, and the darkness Night. And there was evening and there was morning, one day.

God said: "Let there be a firmament in the midst of the water, and let it separate water from water." God made the firmament, and it separated the water that was below the firmament from the water that was above the firmament.

God called the firmament Sky. And there was evening and there was morning, a second day.

God said: "Let the water below the sky be gathered together unto one place, and let the dry land appear." God called the dry land Earth, and the gathering of waters Seas. And God said: "Let the earth put forth grass, herb-bearing seed, and fruit trees of every kind bearing fruit with the seed in it, upon the earth." And the earth brought forth grass, herb-yielding seed after its kind, and fruit trees of every kind bearing fruit with the seed in it. And God saw that it was good. And there was evening and there was morning, a third day.

God said: "Let there be lights in the firmament of the sky to separate day from night; they shall serve as signs for the seasons, and for the days and the years; and they shall serve as light in the firmament of the sky to give light upon the earth." God made the two great lights, the greater light to rule the day, and the lesser light to rule the night, and the stars. And God set them in the firmament of the sky to give light upon the earth, and to rule over the day

and over the night, and to separate the light from darkness; and God saw that it was good. And there was evening and there was morning, a fourth day.

God said: "Let the waters abound with swarms of living creatures, and let birds fly above the earth in the open firmament of Sky." God created the great sea monsters, and all the living creatures of every kind that creep, which the waters brought forth in swarms; and all the winged birds of every kind. And God saw that it was good. God blessed them, saying: "Be fruitful and multiply, fill the waters in the seas, and let the birds multiply on the earth." And there was evening and there was morning, a fifth day.

God said: "Let the earth bring forth every kind of living creature: cattle, creeping things, and wild beasts of every kind." So God made wild beasts of every kind and cattle of every kind, and all kinds of creeping things of the earth. And God saw that it was good. And God said: "Let us make human beings in our image, after our likeness. They shall take care of the fish of the sea, the birds of the sky, the cattle, the whole earth, and all the creeping things that creep on earth." And God created a human in God's own image, in the image of the Holy One, God created a man and a woman. God blessed them and said: "Be fruitful and multiply, fill the earth and repair it; and take care of the fish of the sea, the birds of the sky, and all the living things that creep on earth."

God said: "See, I give you every seed-bearing plant that is upon all the earth, and every tree that has seed-bearing fruit; they shall be yours for food." And it was so. And God saw the whole world, and found it was very good. And there was evening and there was morning, the sixth day.

CHAPTER TWO

And the heaven and the earth were finished, with all their order. On the seventh day God finished making the world, and rested on the seventh day from all the work. And God blessed the seventh day and declared it holy, because on that day the Holy One rested from all the work of creation. Such is the story of heaven and earth when they were created.

Lighting the Candles

The creation of the world is remembered with the lighting of the Shabbat candles. The candles should be lit eighteen minutes before sundown because eighteen is a special number. It means "life" in Hebrew. All Jewish holidays begin at sundown because the world began in darkness. Women usually light the candles, but anyone can do it. Light at least two candles because the Bible has two versions of the commandment to keep the Sabbath: "Remember the Shabbat" (Exodus 20:8) and "Observe the Shabbat" (Deuteronomy 5:12). Some families light a candle for every member of the family.

Cover your head before you light the candles, to show your respect for God. Then light the candles and cover your eyes with your hands. The reason for this is a little confusing. You must light the candles before the blessing because once the prayer is said, Shabbat has begun and fires may no longer be lit. But all blessings must be said before the commandment is done, so you have to cover your eyes in order not to see the candles already lit.

Make three circular motions with your hands over the candles, as though you are bringing the Shabbat into you. Put your hands in front of your eyes and recite the blessing. You can also add your own private prayer silently. Afterward, you might look at the clear, peaceful flames of the candles, think about the past week, take a deep breath, and feel the spirit of Shabbat enter you.

BLESSING

Praised are You, Adonai our God, Ruler of the Universe, who has sanctified our lives through Your commandments, commanding us to kindle the Sabbath lights.

Baruh atah adonai, eloheinu meleh ha-olam, asher kidushanu b'mitzvotav vitzivanu l'hadlik ner shel shabbat.

164

Kiddush

Kiddush, which means "holy," is sung on the eve of every holiday and Shabbat. Usually it is said over wine, because "wine gladdens the heart" (Psalm 104:15). You can stand or sit as you raise the wine cup to recite the blessing. Some people slip the stem of the goblet between two fingers and hold the cup in their palm with their fingers curled upward, like the petals of a rose, which represents perfection.

This blessing thanks God for the great delight of Shabbat, for the creation of the world, and for freeing the Jews from slavery in Egypt. After the blessing, pass the cup of wine for everyone to sip.

BLESSING

Praised are You, Adonai our God, Ruler of the Universe, who creates the fruit of the vine.

Praised are You, Adonai our God, Ruler of the Universe, who has sanctified us through Your commandments and has taken delight in us. You have lovingly and gladly given us the holy Shabbat, a reminder of the Creation. Shabbat is the first among the days of sacred assembly that
recall the Exodus from Egypt. You have chosen us, sanctifying us among all people by granting us your holy Shabbat lovingly and gladly. Praised are You, Adonai, who sanctifies Shabbat.

Baruh atah adonai, eloheinu meleh ha-olam, borei pri hagafen. Baruh atah adonai, eloheinu meleh ha-olam, asher kidushanu b'mitzvotav v'ratzah vanu, v'shabbat kodsho b'ahavah uvratzon hinhilanu, zicaron l'ma'aseh v'rehsheet. Ki hu yom t'hilah l'mikra'eh kodesh zeher litzi'at mitzraim. Ki-vanu vaharta v'otanu kidashtah micol-ha-amim, v'shabbat kodsh'ha b'ahavah uv'ratzon hinhaltanu. Baruh atah adonai mikadesh hashabbat.

Hamotzi

This blessing, which immediately follows the kiddush, is said over the hallah. Remember to uncover the bread before saying the prayer. Then pick up the hallah, ask everyone around the table to touch it, and sing or say the blessing together. When it's over, everyone pinches off a piece of bread to eat.

Praised are You, Adonai our God, Ruler of the Universe, who brings forth bread from the earth.

Baruh atah adonai, eloheinu meleh ha-olam, hamotzi lehem meen ha-aretz.

A Sensitive Hallah

The following story is a reminder that it is the day, not the object, that is holy.

A rich businessman wanted to impress his rabbi with how religious he was. He invited the rabbi to his house on Friday night. When it came time to bless the hallah, the businessman's wife forgot to remove the cloth covering the bread.

"How stupid!" the man screamed at his wife. "You know you're supposed to take off the hallah cover right after the blessing over the wine."

The rabbi stopped the man, saying, "The hallah is covered to spare its feelings because the wine is blessed before it. If this is done for a loaf of bread, imagine how much more important it is to spare your wife's feelings!"

The Sabbath Bride

Once there was a beautiful mountain village called Safed, where everyone studied Torah to find the world's deepest meaning. On Friday afternoon the men went to the fields outside the city to greet Shabbat as though the day were a beloved bride. They imagined their "bride" descending on the rays of the setting sun to meet her groom. They dressed in their finest clothes and sang "Lekhah Dodi": "Come, my love, to greet the Sabbath Bride." Just as a groom loves his bride, anticipates her arrival with joy, and wants to embrace her, so the Jewish people are Shabbat's "bridegroom," because they love "her" so much.

The Sabbath has also been called Shabbat Ha-Malka, the Sabbath Queen, as a reminder that the laws of the day must be obeyed.

Mrs. Moskowitz and the Sabbath Candlesticks

by Amy Schwartz

THE MOVING MAN SET DOWN the last box in Mrs. Moskowitz's new apartment and wiped his brow. "That's it, ma'am," he said. "Enjoy your new home."

Mrs. Moskowitz let her cat out of his box. "You call this a home, Fred?" She walked through the kitchen and the bedroom and back to the living room.

"I miss my old house," she said as she sat down. "I miss the flowers in front. I miss the porch in the back. I miss the old bathtub where I used to wash Sophie and Sam when they were small. This apartment will never be a home."

When Mrs. Moskowitz's son came by that evening, the boxes were still unpacked. Sam kissed his mother and handed her a package. "I found this in the basement when I was locking up the old house, Mother. You must have forgotten it."

Mrs. Moskowitz shook the box. Then she opened the lid and took out a sack made of soft white cloth. She untied the sack and pulled out two tarnished candlesticks.

"My Sabbath candlesticks! When you were little, Sam, I polished these until you could see yourself in the reflection. For Shabbat I cleaned the whole house till it sparkled.

"Sam, remember how good the freshly baked hallah smelled? Remember the laughing and singing after supper? Remember how happy we were?"

"Yes," Sam said. "I remember."

Mrs. Moskowitz shook her head. "What memories, Sam, what memories."

The next morning, when Mrs. Moskowitz pulled back the curtains, a ray of sunlight struck the candlesticks. "Look at that, Fred. Aren't they lovely?" When Mrs. Moskowitz did her marketing, she dropped a jar of silver polish in her basket.

After lunch, Mrs. Moskowitz polished the candlesticks. She held Fred up to them. "Can you see yourself, Fred?"

Then she frowned. "It's that table, Fred! How can my beautiful candlesticks stand on such a plain table?"

Mrs. Moskowitz climbed about the many boxes piled on the floor. She tugged at the top flap of the biggest box and sprang it open. She pulled out a dozen sheets, a blue blanket, and a fluffy comforter with feathers coming out at the seams, but she didn't find what she was looking for.

"Oh, Fred, where could it be?" Mrs. Moskowitz muttered as she tucked the comforter into the bed. She rummaged around the box again. "It's . . . here . . . somewhere. . . . Here it is!" Mrs. Moskowitz pulled out a white tablecloth with silver threads dancing around its border.

She took out the tablecloth and laid it on the table. "Fred, come look! It's magnificent!" Mrs. Moskowitz stood back and looked too.

"But, Fred," she said, "how can such beautiful candlesticks, on such a lovely table, stand on such a filthy floor? Where did I put my mop?"

Mrs. Moskowitz unpacked one box after another and finally found her bucket and mop. She scrubbed and mopped the living room floor and the bedroom floor, and then she cleaned the kitchen. She washed the kitchen cabinets and pushed the furniture into place.

Mrs. Moskowitz rubbed her back. "What those candlesticks are putting me through," she groaned. Then she yawned and turned out the light.

In the morning, Mrs. Moskowitz got up early. She watched the light playing on the candlesticks as she brushed her hair. "What this table needs is a bunch of flowers, don't you think, Fred?"

Mrs. Moskowitz put on her hat and coat and walked to the corner. She went into the flower shop and bought a bunch of posies and daisies.

On her way home, Mrs. Moskowitz stopped at the grocery store. She

bought flour, eggs, yeast, and a box of long white candles. At another store she bought a tall bottle of wine.

When she got home, Mrs. Moskowitz unpacked her groceries. "A table with Shabbat candles, a beautiful tablecloth, and such lovely flowers — it's still missing one thing," she said. Mrs. Moskowitz found her old tin recipe box and pulled out a worn card. "Freshly baked hallah — that's what we need."

Mrs. Moskowitz sifted and stirred and kneaded the dough. Then she rolled it into three long rolls and braided them together.

As she worked, Mrs. Moskowitz thought about baking hallah with her mother many years ago. She thought about raising her family in the old house. And she thought about the years still to come.

Mrs. Moskowitz put the two loaves of hallah in a shallow blue dish and put them aside to rise. Then she wiped her hands on her apron. "Just one more thing, Fred."

Mrs. Moskowitz went to the phone and called her son. "Come over tonight, Sam, and bring the family. We'll light the candles and have a Sabbath meal. I'll call Sophie and invite her too."

Then Mrs. Moskowitz lay down for a little nap.

Just before sundown, Sam and his family and Sophie arrived at the door. "*Shabbat shalom!*" Sam said as he walked in. "Why, Mother, just look at this apartment!"

Mrs. Moskowitz picked up Fred. She looked around her. The boxes were all unpacked. Everything was clean and in place. The candlesticks stood shining on the table. The apartment looked beautiful and here was the family to celebrate Shabbat.

Mrs. Moskowitz laughed. "Fred, when did all this happen?" Mrs. Moskowitz turned to her family. "*Shabbat shalom,*" she said. "And welcome . . . to my home."

Hallah: Traditional Shabbat Treat

In Eastern Europe a century ago, most Jews lived hard lives with much work and very little money. For them, food on Shabbat was very important. No matter how poor they were, they put aside something special for Shabbat. A typical Friday dinner might be chicken soup, gefilte fish, roasted chicken, kugel (noodle pudding), and hallah, the traditional Shabbat bread.

Bread was a large part of a poor person's diet because it was cheap and plentiful. Everyday bread was coarse, chewy, and dark. By contrast, hallah was as splendidly different as Shabbat was from the other days of the week. Made from precious white flour and eggs, it is yellow-white, fluffy, and sweet.

Hallah (the word means "dough" in Hebrew) is still a treat, especially home-baked hallah. Besides being a delicious part of the Shabbat dinner, its fragrance while baking helps set the mood for Shabbat. It's also fun to make the braids that form the shape of the bread.

Some people have two loaves of hallah to express the feeling of abundance on Shabbat and as a reminder of God's help in the wilderness. When the Israelites wandered in the desert, they found manna, a white edible plant that grew where nothing else did. The Israelites always found enough manna to gather for one day. On Friday they found enough manna for two days, so they picked a double portion. No manna appeared on Shabbat. From this experience the Israelites learned not to gather food on Shabbat.

The hallah is covered with a pretty cloth during the kiddush to spare its feelings in being blessed after the wine. When it's time to bless the hallah, the cover is taken off. After the blessing, everyone tears off rather than cuts a piece of hallah, because knives are not part of a day that celebrates love.

Hallah

Note that hallah has seven ingredients, the number of completion and perfection. You can add an eighth ingredient, such as raisins, sesame seeds, or poppy seeds, for extra flavor.

1 package dry yeast

1 cup warm water (98°F)

1 teaspoon salt

2 tablespoons sugar

3 eggs

2 teaspoons vegetable oil

3 ½ cups white flour, preferably unbleached

¼ cup poppy or sesame seeds (optional)

¼ cup raisins (optional)

Pour the yeast into a large bowl, and mix in the warm water until the yeast is dissolved. Add the salt and sugar, and stir until they dissolve. Lightly beat in two of the eggs and the oil. Slowly add three cups of the flour, stirring it into the liquid.

Sprinkle a large cutting board with the remaining half-cup of flour, and put the dough on it. Knead the dough by pressing the heel of your hand into its center. Then fold the dough in half, and keep kneading it for another few minutes. Kneading makes the bread springy and light. Put the dough back into the bowl and cover it with a damp cloth to keep the surface from getting dry.

Let the dough rise for at least two hours. Preheat the oven to 350°F. After the dough has risen to twice its original size, punch it down. Add the raisins. Put the dough on a lightly floured cutting board, and divide it into quarters. Take three quarters and roll each into a long snake. Line up the snakes next to one another and braid them.

Take the last quarter and divide it into thirds, making three smaller snakes. Braid it the same way, and put it on top of the larger braid. Put on a cookie sheet. Separate the yolk from the white of the third egg and, with your fingers, paint the surface of the dough with yolk. Sprinkle the loaf with poppy or sesame seeds, and bake for 45 minutes.

 # *Glossary*

afikomen: "dessert"; the broken piece of matzah put aside at the beginning of the seder and eaten at the end of the meal.

aravot: willows; one of the four species used during Sukkot.

arb'ah minim: the four species, or plants, used during Sukkot.

B.C.E.: Before the Common Era. Christians use the term B.C. (Before Christ).

ba'al teki'ah: master of the shofar; shofar blower.

beitzah: the roasted egg on the seder plate, which symbolizes the ancient festival animal sacrifice.

Bereshit: the first book of the five books of the Torah; also called Genesis.

C.E.: Common Era. Christians use the term A.D. (Anno Domini, which means "in the year of the Lord").

dreidel: a spinning top used in Hanukkah games.

Elul: the month before Tishri.

Eretz Israel: Land of Israel.

etrog: a citron; one of the four species used during Sukkot.

falafel: Middle Eastern "fast food" made with chickpeas.

gefilte fish: stuffed fish.

gelt: money traditionally given during Hanukkah.

gimel: Hebrew letter found on the dreidel.

grogger: noisemaker used to drown out Haman's name during the reading of the Megillah.

hadasim: myrtle; one of the four species used during Sukkot.

Hadassah: Esther's Hebrew name, which means myrtle, a beautiful plant.

Haggadah: the special book read at the seder that tells the story of Passover and the meaning of the food on the table; "the telling."

hallah: an egg bread eaten on Shabbat and other Jewish festivals.

hamantaschen: triangular cookies filled with fruit, eaten on Purim; "Haman's pockets."

hametz: leavened bread and food, as well as dishes and cooking utensils used throughout the year, which cannot be used at Passover.

Hamotzi: blessing said over the hallah on Shabbat.

hanukkiyah: a candelabrum with nine branches used for Hanukkah.

haroset: a mixture of apples, nuts, wine, and cinnamon eaten at the seder in remembrance of the mortar used by the Israelite slaves to build Egyptian cities.

he: Hebrew letter found on the dreidel.

He-Hag: Hebrew for "the Holiday"; another name for Sukkot.

imberlah: cookie dough.

karpas: fresh greens, such as parsley, celery, or lettuce, eaten during the seder to symbolize springtime.

kibbutz: a farm community in Israel where everyone works and everyone shares property.

kiddush: the blessing for the Sabbath and holidays, said over wine.

kiddushin: holiness.

Kislev: ninth month of the Hebrew calendar.

Kohen: one of the three remaining tribes of Israel.

Kol Nidre: prayer said on the holiest night of the year, the eve of Yom Kippur; "All Vows."

kugel: noodle pudding.

latke: potato pancake fried in oil.

Levi: one of the three remaining tribes of Israel.

lulav: a date palm; one of the four species used during Sukkot.

Maccabee: refers to Judah and his family, who led the struggle against King Antiochus IV; also means "hammer."

Magen David: Star, or Shield, of David; six-pointed star that has become a symbol of Judaism.

manna: the special food God gave the Jews when they were in the desert for forty years; probably a plant that enabled them to survive.

maror: bitter herbs, often horseradish, eaten at the seder to remember the bitterness of the Israelites during Egyptian bondage.

matzah: unleavened bread.

Megillah: scroll that tells the story of Esther (Megillat Esther) and is read at Purim.

menorah: a candelabrum used for religious purposes. A Hanukkah menorah has nine branches; a synagogue menorah has seven branches.

Messiah: the redeemer, or savior, who waits for the world to be ready for the Holy Presence.

midrash: a story or legend that has its beginnings in the Torah; often it explains some part of the Torah.

mishloah manot: the sending of gifts; little plates of sweets that friends give to one another during Purim.

mitzvah: something God commands a person to do; a good deed.

mondel bread: sweet, hard bread.

Ne'ilah: last service on Yom Kippur; "Closing the Gates."

Nisan: the first month of the Jewish calendar; the month in which Passover falls.

nun: Hebrew letter found on the dreidel.

omer: a sheaf of barley.

Palestine: the name for Israel before 1948.

sabra: native Israeli.

Safed: a city in Israel where the Cabalists lived.

Sambatyon: a mythical river that flowed for six days and rested on the seventh. It offered protection to the Jewish people.

seder: "order"; a dinner with special foods and a ceremony.

Shabbat Ha-Malka: the Sabbath Queen.

shammash: the "servant" candle of the *hanukkiyah,* used to light the eight Hanukkah candles.

Shema: the holiest Jewish prayer: "Hear, O Israel, the Lord our God, the Lord is One."

shevarim: three short blasts blown on the shofar during Rosh Hashanah.

Shevat: month in which Tu B'Sh'vat falls; usually late January or February.

shin: Hebrew letter found on the dreidel.

shmurah matzah: guarded matzah.

shofar: trumpet made from a ram's horn and blown during the High Holy Days.

sukkah: little temporary hut in which to celebrate Sukkot.

Talmud: the body of Jewish civil and ceremonial law interpreted through the Torah.

tefillah: prayer.

teki'ah: long, clear blast blown on the shofar during Rosh Hashanah.

teki'ah gedolah: final, long blast blown on the shofar at the end of Rosh Hashanah and Yom Kippur.

teru'ah: nine very fast, short blasts blown on the shofar during Rosh Hashanah.

teshuvah: returning to God; self-examination.

Tishri: Hebrew month in which Rosh Hashanah and Yom Kippur fall.

Torah: the first five books of the Bible; all learning, direction; also called the tree of life.

tsimmis: carrots cooked with honey and raisins.

tzedakah: giving to those in need; justice.

ushpizin: invisible guests who are invited to visit the sukkah.

Yisrael: one of the three remaining tribes of Israel.

Yom Teru'ah: Day of Blowing the Shofar; another name for Rosh Hashanah.

Zeman Mattan Torahtenu: the Time of the Giving of Our Torah; a name for Shavuot.

Zion: an ancient name for Israel.

z'roah: a roasted shank bone; appears on the seder plate as a reminder of the lamb sacrificed by the Israelites; also a symbol of the outstretched arm of God to take them out of Egypt.

Illustrator's Notes

The borders of each chapter's opening pages were greatly influenced by Hebrew illuminated manuscript paintings. The clothes of the figures reflect those worn by Jews across the ages in various parts of the world.

Rosh Hashanah and Yom Kippur: The clothes are Italian, from the late eighteenth century, adapted from a painting celebrating a circumcision in Venice. The border, with gold balls typical of many Italian Renaissance manuscripts, was adapted from a page in the *Rothschild Mahzor,* Italy, 1492.

Sukkot: The clothes are Austrian, from the eighteenth century. The border was adapted from a Haggadah illuminated by Joel ben Simeon, Germany and northern Italy, mid—fifteenth century. The pumpkins and cranberries are distinctly American.

Hanukkah: The early eighteenth-century German menorah has the traditional flowers-and-buttons design of the original candelabrum in the Great Temple. The clothes are from nineteenth-century Poland, and the border was adapted from the *Rothschild Mahzor,* Italy, 1492.

Tu B'Sh'vat: The clothes were influenced by a fifth-century mosaic of Abraham and Sarah in Santa Maria Maggiore, Rome. The olive trees were adapted from a miniature in the Cervera Bible, Spain, 1300.

Purim: The children wear the clothes of nineteenth-century Algeria and Morocco. Almost all of the borders were composed from designs on nineteenth-century Persian and Tunisian *ketubot,* traditional marriage documents.

Pesah: The clothes are German, from the mid—fifteenth century. Notice the yellow "Jew's hat" and Jewish badges, some form of which Jews were ordered to wear at different times in different countries. The border was found on a nineteenth-century *ketuba* from Jerusalem.

Shabbat: The border was adapted from the doors of the Ark of the Covenant, Scuola Grande Tedesca, Ghetto Nuovo, Venice, Italy, 1672. The crown appears in the *Rothschild Mahzor,* Italy, 1492.

For Further Reading

Burstein, Chaya. *A Kid's Catalog of Israel.* Philadelphia: Jewish Publication Society, 1988.

Drucker, Malka and Gay Block. *Rescuers: Portraits of Moral Courage in the Holocaust.* New York: Holmes and Meier, 1992.

Drucker, Malka and Michael Halperin. *Jacob's Rescue: A Holocaust Story.* New York: Bantam, 1993.

Frank, Anne. *Anne Frank: Diary of a Young Girl.* New York: Doubleday, 1990.

Greenberg, Irving. *The Jewish Way: Living the Holidays.* New York: Summit Books, 1988.

Plaut, Gunther T. *The Torah: A Modern Commentary.* New York: Union of American Hebrew Congregations, 1981.

Prague, Artia. *I Never Saw Another Butterfly.* New York: Schocken, 1993.

Strassfeld, Michael. *The Jewish Holidays.* New York: Harper and Row, 1985.

Weilerstein, Sadie Rose. *The Adventures of K'Tonton.* New York: Women's League for Conservative Judaism, 1977.

Also by the Author

Celebrating Life: Jewish Rites of Passage. New York: Holiday House, 1984.

Eliezer Ben-Yehuda: Father of Modern Hebrew. New York: Dutton, 1987.

Grandma's Latkes. New York: Harcourt Brace, 1992.

Hanukkah: Eight Nights, Eight Lights. New York: Holiday House, 1980.

A Jewish Holiday ABC. New York: Harcourt Brace, 1992

Passover: A Season of Freedom. New York: Holiday House, 1981.

Rosh Hashanah and Yom Kippur: Sweet Beginnings. New York: Holiday House, 1982.

Shabbat: A Peaceful Island. New York: Holiday House, 1984.

Sukkot: A Time to Rejoice. New York: Holiday House, 1983.

 # *Index*

Acknowledgments

"Maybe Even Higher" retold by the author from "If Not Higher," by I. L. Peretz.

The author is grateful to the following for granting permission to include copyrighted material in this collection:

Adler, David: *The House on the Roof.* Copyright © 1976 by David Adler. Reprinted by permission of Kar-Ben Copies, Inc.

Bulla, Clyde Robert: *Jonah and the Great Fish.* Copyright © 1970 by Clyde Robert Bulla. Reprinted by permission of HarperCollins Publishers.

Cohen, Barbara: *The Carp in the Bathtub.* Copyright © 1972 by Barbara Cohen. Reprinted by permission of Lothrop, Lee & Shepard Books, a division of William Morrow and Company, Inc.

cummings, e. e.: "i thank You God for most this amazing" from *Complete Poems, 1904–1962,* by e. e. cummings, edited by George J. Firmage. Copyright 1950, ©1978, 1991 by the Trustees for the e. e. cummings Trust. Copyright ©1979 by George J. Firmage. Reprinted by permission of Liveright Publishing Corporation.

Frank, Anne: Selections from *Anne Frank: Diary of a Young Girl.* Copyright 1952 by Otto H. Frank. Reprinted by permission of Doubleday, a division of Random House, Inc.

Friedman, Deborah Lynn: "The 613 Commandments." Copyright © 1983 by Deborah Lynn Friedman (ASCAP). Abridged and reprinted by permission of Deborah Lynn Friedman (ASCAP)/Sounds Write Productions, Inc. (ASCAP).

Friedman, Deborah Lynn: "The Tu B'Sh'vat Song." Copyright © 1993 by Deborah Lynn Friedman (ASCAP). Reprinted by permission of Deborah Lynn Friedman (ASCAP)/Sounds Write Productions, Inc. (ASCAP).

Hetkin, Shalom: "Brothers" from *The World Over Story Book,* by Shalom Hetkin. Copyright 1954 by Shalom Hetkin. Adapted by the author by permission of the Board of Jewish Education of Greater New York.

Livingston, Myra Cohn: "I'm Sorry" from *The Way Things Are and Other Poems,* by Myra Cohn Livingston. Copyright © 1974 by Myra Cohn Livingston. Reprinted by permission of Marian Reiner for the author.

Prague, Artia: "Homesick," "At Terezin," and "On a Sunny Evening" from *I Never Saw Another Butterfly* (Expanded 2nd Edition), by the U.S. Holocaust Memorial Council, edited by Hana Volavkova. Copyright © 1978, 1993 by Artia Prague. Compilation © 1993 by Schocken Books Inc. Reprinted by permission of Schocken Books, distributed by Pantheon Books, a division of Random House, Inc.

Singer, Isaac Bashevis: "Zlateh the Goat" from *Zlateh the Goat and Other Stories,* by Isaac Bashevis Singer. Copyright © 1966 by Isaac Bashevis Singer. Reprinted by permission of HarperCollins Publishers.

Schwartz, Amy: *Mrs. Moskowitz and the Sabbath Candlesticks.* Copyright © 1983 by Amy Schwartz. Reprinted by permission of Jewish Publication Society.

Udry, Janice May: *A Tree Is Nice.* Copyright © 1956 by Janice May Udry. Copyright © renewed 1984 by Janice May Udry. Reprinted by permission of HarperCollins Publishers.

Weilerstein, Sadie Rose: "How K'Tonton Masqueraded on Purim" from *The Adventures of K'Tonton,* by Sadie Rose Weilerstein. Copyright © 1977 by Sadie Rose Weilerstein. Reprinted by permission of Women's League for Conservative Judaism.

Wolfson, Dr. Ron: Pesah Pillow Placecards, Haroset recipe, and The Onomatopoeic "Had Gadya" from *The Art of Jewish Living: The Passover Seder.* (Woodstock, Vt.: Jewish Lights Publishing, 1996). © 1988 by The Federation of Jewish Men's Clubs. $16.95 + $3.50 s/h. Order by mail or call 800-962-4544. Permission granted by Jewish Lights Publishing, P.O. Box 237, Woodstock, Vt. 05091.